BUILDING
HISTORY
SERIES

MACHU
PICCHU

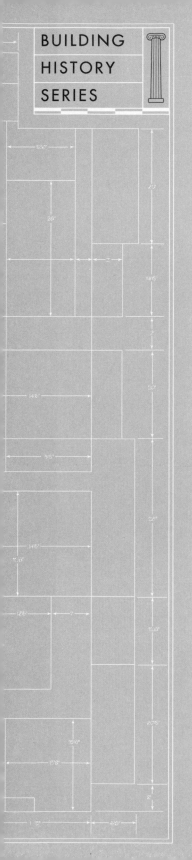

MACHU
PICCHU

TITLES IN THE BUILDING HISTORY SERIES INCLUDE:

Alcatraz
The Atom Bomb
The Eiffel Tower
The Golden Gate Bridge
The Great Wall of China
The Holy City of Jerusalem
The Medieval Castle
The Medieval Cathedral
Mount Rushmore
The New York Subway System
The Palace of Versailles
The Panama Canal
The Parthenon of Ancient Greece
The Pyramids of Giza
The Roman Colosseum
Roman Roads and Aqueducts
The Russian Kremlin
Shakespeare's Globe
The Sistine Chapel
The Space Shuttle
The Statue of Liberty
Stonehenge
The Suez Canal
The Taj Mahal
The Titanic
The Tower of Pisa
The Transcontinental Railroad
The Viking Longship
The White House
The World Trade Center

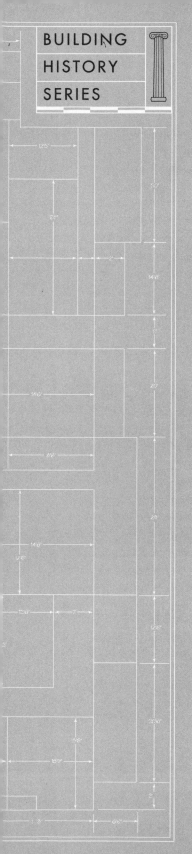

BUILDING
HISTORY
SERIES

MACHU
PICCHU

by Amy Allison

LUCENT
BOOKS®

THOMSON

GALE

Detroit • New York • San Diego • San Francisco
Boston • New Haven, Conn. • Waterville, Maine
London • Munich

LIBRARY OF CONGRESS CATALOGING-IN-PUBLICATION DATA

Allison, Amy, 1956–
    Machu Picchu / by Amy Allison.
        p.   cm. — (Building history series)
Includes bibliographical references and index.
Summary: Describes the ancient Incan city of Machu Picchu, the ruins of which show
the religious beliefs, masterful stonework, wise use of natural resources, and history of
the people who ruled the largest indigenous empire of the Americas.
        ISBN 1-59018-020-8 (hardback: alk. paper)
        1. Machu Picchu Site (Peru)—Juvenile literature.   2. Inca architecture—Juvenile
literature.   [1. Machu Picchu Site (Peru)   2. Incas.   3. Indians of South America.
4. Architecture.]   I. Title.   II. Series.
    F3429.1.M3 A5 2003
    985'.37—dc21

                                                                              2001007309

CONTENTS

FOREWORD

Throughout history, as civilizations have evolved and prospered, each has produced unique buildings and architectural styles. Combining the need for both utility and artistic expression, a society's buildings, particularly its large-scale public structures, often reflect the individual character traits that distinguish it from other societies. In a very real sense, then, buildings express a society's values and unique characteristics in tangible form. As scholar Anita Abramovitz comments in her book *People and Spaces*, "Our ways of living and thinking—our habits, needs, fear of enemies, aspirations, materialistic concerns, and religious beliefs—have influenced the kinds of spaces that we build and that later surround and include us."

That specific types and styles of structures constitute an outward expression of the spirit of an individual people or era can be seen in the diverse ways that various societies have built palaces, fortresses, tombs, churches, government buildings, sports arenas, public works, and other such monuments. The ancient Greeks, for instance, were a supremely rational people who originated Western philosophy and science, including the atomic theory and the realization that the earth is a sphere. Their public buildings, epitomized by Athens's magnificent Parthenon temple, were equally rational, emphasizing order, harmony, reason, and above all, restraint.

By contrast, the Romans, who conquered and absorbed the Greek lands, were a highly practical people preoccupied with acquiring and wielding power over others. The Romans greatly admired and readily copied elements of Greek architecture, but modified and adapted them to their own needs. "Roman genius was called into action by the enormous practical needs of a world empire," wrote historian Edith Hamilton. "Rome met them magnificently. Buildings tremendous, indomitable, amphitheaters where eighty thousand could watch a spectacle, baths where three thousand could bathe at the same time."

In medieval Europe, God heavily influenced and motivated the people, and religion permeated all aspects of society, molding people's worldviews and guiding their everyday actions. That spiritual mindset is reflected in the most important medieval structure—the Gothic cathedral—which, in a sense, was a model of heavenly cities. As scholar Anne Fremantle so elegantly phrases it, the cathedrals were "harmonious elevations of stone and glass reaching up to heaven to seek and receive the light [of God]."

Our more secular modern age, in contrast, is driven by the realities of a global economy, advanced technology, and mass communications. Responding to the needs of international trade and the growth of cities housing millions of people, today's builders construct engineering marvels, among them towering skyscrapers of steel and glass, mammoth marine canals, and huge and elaborate rapid transit systems, all of which would have left their ancestors, even the Romans, awestruck.

In examining some of humanity's greatest edifices, Lucent Books' Building History series recognizes this close relationship between a society's historical character and its buildings. Each volume in the series begins with a historical sketch of the people who erected the edifice, exploring their major achievements as well as the beliefs, customs, and societal needs that dictated the variety, functions, and styles of their buildings. A detailed explanation of how the selected structure was conceived, designed, and built, to the extent that this information is known, makes up the majority of the volume.

Each volume in the Lucent Building History series also includes several special features that are useful tools for additional research. A chronology of important dates gives students an overview, at a glance, of the evolution and use of the structure described. Sidebars create a broader context by adding further details on some of the architects, engineers, and construction tools, materials, and methods that made each structure a reality, as well as the social, political, and/or religious leaders and movements that inspired its creation. Useful maps help the reader locate the nations, cities, streets, and individual structures mentioned in the text; and numerous diagrams and pictures illustrate tools and devices that bring to life various stages of construction. Finally, each volume contains two bibliographies, one for student research, the other listing works the author consulted in compiling the book.

Taken as a whole, these volumes, covering diverse ancient and modern structures, constitute not only a valuable research tool, but also a tribute to the human spirit, a fascinating exploration of the dreams, skills, ingenuity, and dogged determination of the great peoples who shaped history.

Important Dates in the History of Machu Picchu

1200
The Incas establish themselves in Cuzco.

1860s
Peruvian geographer Antonio Raimondi maps much of the country's remote areas.

1438
Inca Pachacuti's victory over the Chanca tribe launches the Inca Empire.

1534
The Inca capital of Cuzco, and with it the empire, falls to Spaniard Francisco Pizarro and his band of conquistadors; by this time, Machu Picchu was probably abandoned.

1200   **1500**   **1800**

c. 1450
Construction begins on Machu Picchu.

1539
The Spanish conquistadors crush a rebellion by the Incas, decisively ending their rule.

1532
Spanish conquistadors begin invading the Inca empire.

1528
Inca Huayna Capac's death, apparently from smallpox brought to America by Europeans, leads to civil war as his two sons fight for control of the empire.

1911
Supplied with Raimondi's maps, Hiram Bingham explores the Urubamba region and uncovers the ruins of Machu Picchu.

1913
National Geographic magazine publishes Bingham's report of his 1912 expedition; its photographs of Machu Picchu spark the public's interest in visiting the remote location.

2000
UNESCO protests the cable car plan by placing Machu Picchu on its list of the 100 Most Endangered Heritage Sites.

1983
The United Nations Educational, Scientific, and Cultural Organization (UNESCO) declares Machu Picchu a World Heritage Site.

1900   **1950**   **2000**

1912
Bingham leads an expedition, cosponsored by Yale University and the National Geographic Society, to clear and excavate the site.

1999
The Peruvian government endorses a controversial plan for cable car transport to Machu Picchu.

1928
Railroad tracks are laid linking Cuzco to Machu Picchu, increasing tourist travel.

2001
The Peruvian government suspends the cable car plan; UNESCO removes Màchu Picchu from its Most Endangered list.

INTRODUCTION: MUTE WITNESS TO A LOST WORLD

Machu Picchu is one of South America's most famous sites. More than a thousand people a day make the journey to this Inca ruin, perched nearly eight thousand feet above sea level in the Peruvian Andes. A sense of mystery about the place draws visitors, from vacationing tourists to pilgrims seeking a spiritual experience. Mystery, in fact, defines the place, as so little about it is known.

The most likely theory is that Machu Picchu was built as a kind of sanctuary or retreat around A.D. 1450. Archaeologists have identified temples and residences at the remote site, as well as plazas, fountains, and farming terraces, covering a total area of about seventy acres.

SECRET SURVIVOR

Machu Picchu bears witness to the achievements of the Inca people, who never documented them in writing. Yet, even without a written language, the Inca civilization became the most powerful and widespread in America before the arrival of the Europeans. In less than a hundred years, from the fifteenth to the sixteenth century, the Incas created an empire that encompassed today's nations of Ecuador, Peru, Bolivia, Chile, and part of Argentina, ruling over about 10 million people. Its size rivaled that of ancient Rome.

Much of what we read about Inca history and culture comes from chronicles, or reports, written in Spanish by soldiers, priests, and individuals of mixed Inca and Spanish heritage. The chronicles were published following the defeat of the Incas by Spanish forces in the mid-sixteenth century. The chroniclers based their writings on their own observations as well as on interviews with native peoples. Curiously, the chronicles they produced made no reference to Machu Picchu. Its secret was apparently kept by those who fled the site even before Spanish soldiers marched into Inca land, intent on conquest.

WORLD HERITAGE SITE

Machu Picchu is the most extensive, well-preserved Inca ruin so far discovered outside Cuzco, the Inca capital city. The nearly

175 intact Inca buildings on view at Machu Picchu give insight into the architecture, culture, and religion of the Incas.

In recognition of Machu Picchu's historical significance, the United Nations Educational, Scientific, and Cultural Organization (UNESCO) added it to their list of World Heritage Sites in 1983. UNESCO intends the list to promote the preservation of

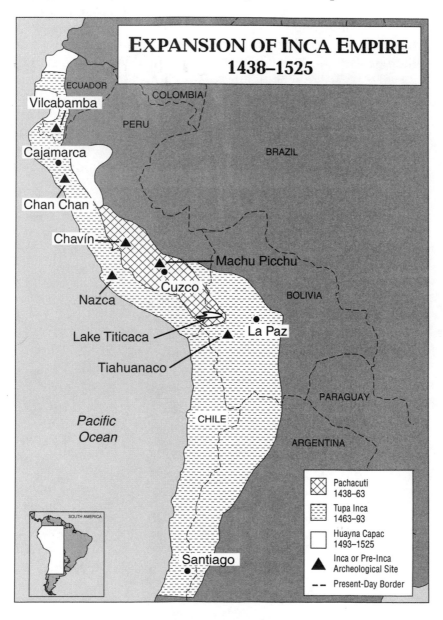

EXPANSION OF INCA EMPIRE
1438–1525

ECUADOR
COLOMBIA
Vilcabamba
PERU
Cajamarca
BRAZIL
Chan Chan
Chavín
Machu Picchu
Cuzco
BOLIVIA
Nazca
Lake Titicaca
La Paz
Tiahuanaco
PARAGUAY
Pacific
Ocean
CHILE
ARGENTINA
SOUTH AMERICA
Santiago

Pachacuti
1438–63

Tupa Inca
1463–93

Huayna Capac
1493–1525

▲ Inca or Pre-Inca
Archeological Site

-- Present-Day Border

buildings, monuments, and natural features that constitute a common heritage for the people of Earth. Machu Picchu has joined Australia's Great Barrier Reef, Greece's Acropolis, England's Stonehenge, and the United States' Grand Canyon—as well as more than seven hundred other sites—named to the list. According to Elías J. Mujica, director of the Andean Institute of Archaeological Studies: "The beauty and exceptional quality of the pre-Hispanic buildings [at Machu Picchu] . . . and the way in which the ancient Peruvians planned and harmonised their buildings with the surrounding site fully justified its inclusion."[1]

UNESCO's World Heritage mission hopes to encourage nations around the world to preserve natural and architectural treasures within their borders. For hundreds of years, the skillful construction of Machu Picchu's stone buildings protected them from the threat of earthquakes and landslides and the encroachment of jungle growth. These remarkable buildings continue to dazzle visitors to the site. Yet Machu Picchu's appeal to

Machu Picchu was named a World Heritage Site in 1983, and continues to attract visitors from around the world.

Machu Picchu's buildings, like the royal tomb shown here, give insight into the architecture, culture, and religion of the Incas.

travelers is proving to be a mixed blessing. Along with tourist dollars come crowding and pollution, which risk marring the unique beauty of the place. Today the challenge facing Peru's government, as stewards of Machu Picchu, is to balance the tourist income the ruins bring to a poor nation with the call to safeguard the site for future generations.

RECLAIMED FROM THE JUNGLE

The ruins known as Machu Picchu lie along a ridge separating the peaks of Machu Picchu and Huayna Picchu (meaning, respectively, "old peak" or "bigger peak," and "young peak" or "smaller peak," in the native Quechua language). The site is divided into an agricultural sector and an urban sector. The urban sector is divided still further, into eastern and western portions. Linking the two urban portions is a large, football field–sized plaza. Ceremonies and other social gatherings, possibly including a sporting event similar to field hockey, took place at this shared open space.

The western, more elevated, urban area is known as the *hanan*, or upper half, and the eastern the *hurin*, or lower half. According to chronicler Bernabé Cobo, the Incas "divided every town or chiefdom into two sections or groups known as hanansaya and hurinsaya, which mean the upper ward and lower ward."[2] At Machu Picchu the *hanan* section generally features the site's most high-quality stonework, while humbler buildings are concentrated in the lower ward.

HANANSAYA

A flight of fountains, paralleled by a stone staircase, descends from the *hanansaya* to the *hurinsaya* of Machu Picchu. The first seven fountains belong to the upper ward, the remaining nine to the lower.

South of the third fountain is a spectacular circular tower sometimes called the Torréon (meaning "tower" in Spanish). This structure forms part of a complex that may have served as a temple honoring the Inca sun god, Inti.

Northwest of the Torréon, at the head of the fountains, a group of buildings is distinguished by the solidity and artistry of their stonework. A massive stone lintel, weighing about three tons, tops the main door to this compound, which has been identified as Machu Picchu's royal residence.

Farther north lies a plaza called the Sacred Plaza because it is bordered by two monumental buildings believed to have been Inca temples. One is considered to be Machu Picchu's principal temple, devoted to the creator god, Viracocha. The other, one of the site's most mysterious buildings, is known as the Temple of the Three Windows.

Just north of the Sacred Plaza, a series of stone steps leads to Machu Picchu's highest point. Here the Incas carved a stepped platform, known as the Intihuatana, from a single block of granite. No one knows for sure the ceremony staged at this platform, but it must have been important, given the care with which the stone block has been shaped and the dramatic view it commands. From the Intihuatana, one can see the whole of Machu Picchu, along with its encircling peaks.

HURINSAYA

Across the main plaza from the Intihuatana lies what was probably Machu Picchu's main residential area. Small dwellings as well as a large barrackslike structure are found among the buildings here, at the site's northeast end.

To the south stands a group of buildings known as the Industrial Group or the Mortar Group. Two hollowed-out stones resembling mortars, or bowls, set into the floor of one of the buildings in the group suggest it was a work area. Some argue,

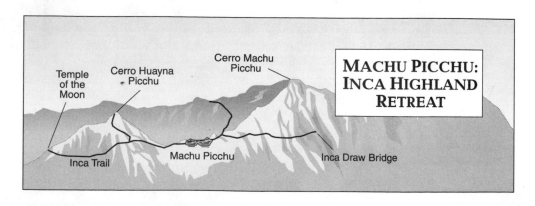

Temple of the Moon

Cerro Huayna Picchu

Cerro Machu Picchu

Inca Trail

Machu Picchu

Inca Draw Bridge

MACHU PICCHU: INCA HIGHLAND RETREAT

The mysterious Temple of the Three Windows is part of Machu Picchu's Sacred Plaza.

however, that these stones were not mortars at all but instead served some ceremonial or ritual purpose.

A group of buildings farther south, highlighted by a condor-shaped stone, has also sparked debate. Andean peoples have long revered the condor, South America's largest bird, which is able to fly to great heights. In fact, the Incas thought condors embodied the spirits of sacred mountains, which themselves soar high in the sky. They also believed the condor, which is a type of vulture, conducted the souls of the dead to the land of their ancestors. Based in part on the condor's multiple symbolic meanings for the architects of Machu Picchu, some see this group of buildings as a temple complex, others as a prison where death sentences were carried out. This debate, like most swirling about Machu Picchu, may never be resolved.

THREATENED BY NATURE

The purpose each of its buildings served is only one of the mysteries that Machu Picchu poses for historians and archaeologists.

Possibly the most persistent mystery surrounding Machu Picchu concerns its abandonment by the Incas. Although historians seem fairly certain its population quit the site sometime in the early sixteenth century, they cannot say for sure why. Natural disaster, disease, and warfare may all be reasons why Machu Picchu was deserted.

Some scholars blame a natural disaster for Machu Picchu's abandonment. Indeed, geologic faults surround the site, making it prone to earthquakes and landslides. Fires have also swept the area, as indicated by a crack above the doorway of one building, caused by the heat of fire. Machu Picchu's stone structures may have withstood the blaze, but many of its inhabitants may not have escaped the smoke and flames.

Others theorize that an insufficient water supply forced residents to leave. Investigation has shown a branch of the main water canal still under construction, suggesting that an effort was under way to increase the flow of water to Machu Picchu. Interruption of the branch canal project may well have led to the city's abandonment. In the dry season, mountain springs feeding the existing canal would have failed to provide enough water for residents, especially when Machu Picchu's population swelled to its estimated maximum of twelve hundred. Drought would have also emptied the reservoirs downhill from the sanctuary, relying as they did on groundwater flow which, in turn, depended on rainfall. Water would have had to be carried in large jars up from the Urubamba River, more than fifteen hundred feet below, which offered a great challenge, if not an impossibility.

DEVASTATED BY DISEASE

Machu Picchu's branch canal project may have been interrupted because construction crews were wiped out by disease. Beginning in the sixteenth century, a deadly epidemic devastated the Inca population. Historians trace this epidemic to the arrival of Europeans in America. The newcomers brought with them diseases against which the native people had no immunity. One of these diseases, probably smallpox, spread southward into Inca territory from Panama possibly as early as 1511, when Spaniards established a settlement there. By 1532, when Spanish conquistadors began their invasion of the Inca Empire, nearly half the native population had been felled by disease. Not even Huayna

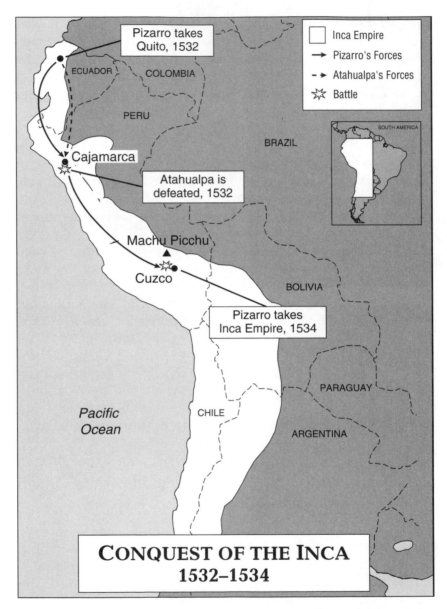

Inca Empire
→ Pizarro's Forces
⇢ Atahualpa's Forces
✻ Battle

Pizarro takes
Quito, 1532

ECUADOR   COLOMBIA

PERU

BRAZIL

SOUTH AMERICA

Cajamarca

Atahualpa is
defeated, 1532

Machu Picchu

Cuzco

BOLIVIA

Pizarro takes
Inca Empire, 1534

PARAGUAY

Pacific
Ocean

CHILE

ARGENTINA

CONQUEST OF THE INCA
1532–1534

Capac, the Sapa, or Supreme Inca, was spared. He died a victim of the epidemic in 1528.

A CASUALTY OF WAR

Some scholars point to the civil war that broke out after Huayna Capac succumbed to the epidemic as the reason Machu Picchu was abandoned. After the death of the Sapa Inca, his two sons,

Huáscar and Atahuallpa, battled each other for the throne. Labor crews at Machu Picchu would have eventually been forced to abandon their work at the site and serve as soldiers in the war between the brothers.

Whether Machu Picchu lost its work crews to disease or warfare, or both, the community could not sustain itself for long without forced labor to provide its upkeep. Trails and bridges leading to its remote location would have soon fallen into disrepair, making the route to Machu Picchu impassable. An overgrowth of weeds, vines, and brambles, along with seasonal landslides, would have eventually blocked any approach to the settlement.

LOST TO THE WORLD

During Machu Picchu's existence, tight restrictions on travel along Inca roads preserved its isolation. Chances are that only a

Spanish conquistador Hernando de Soto (left) stands at the side of the Sapa Inca in this late-nineteenth-century painting.

privileged few, such as members of the royal family and trusted record keepers, would have been able to locate the remote site following its abandonment. Once this select group of individuals, and any surviving inhabitants, became adrift in the chaos following the collapse of the Inca Empire, knowledge of the site was lost to the rest of the world.

Machu Picchu could never be known through books or written records produced by the Incas, because they never developed a written language. Instead, their record keeping involved a kind of memory aid called a *quipu*, which consisted of an arrangement of knotted threads hanging from a cord. The placement and size of the knots, as well as the color of the thread, coded information of value to the empire. A *quipu* kept track of such details as the number of supplies in a storehouse or the time it took to travel from one place to another. Historical events were documented, too, for example, the succession of Inca rulers. A special class of individuals, called the *quipucamaya* (meaning "he who has charge of the accounts"), was trained to interpret these devices.

With the breakup of the state following civil war, the Incas' system of storing and retrieving information fell into disarray. The orderly world where the *quipucamayas* played a part had shattered beyond repair. Any record of Machu Picchu vanished along with the *quipus* that documented its existence and the *quipucamayas* who could interpret them.

Because of the general population's ignorance of Machu Picchu, the Spanish conquistadors never learned of its existence when they conquered the Inca Empire in 1534. Indeed, no mention of the sanctuary appears in the writings of the Spanish chroniclers, from whom we have the most-detailed reports of Inca culture.

The fact that the Spanish conquistadors had no knowledge of Machu Picchu was probably its saving grace. In the name of Christianity, the conquistadors destroyed Inca shrines to their gods—which would have included much of Machu Picchu. Greed also played a part in the defacement of these shrines, as they were often adorned with gold. The Spaniards would have robbed them of their gold, eager for the riches this precious metal would bring when shipped back home.

Only jungle plants invaded the site, and Machu Picchu survived their encroachment remarkably well. Thanks to the skill

EL DORADO

Tales of a fabulously wealthy kingdom to the south began circulating among Spanish settlers in Panama around 1511. A native chieftain passed these tales on to the greedy Spaniards in an attempt to get rid of them. The tales were based on reports of Inca gold. The Spaniards spoke of the rumored kingdom as El Dorado, meaning "The Gilded" in Spanish.

In 1532 the fortune hunter Francisco Pizarro marched into Inca territory in his search for El Dorado. Fortunately for Pizarro, civil war and a deadly epidemic had weakened the mighty Inca Empire. With a force of less than two hundred men—equipped with firearms and horses, which the Incas lacked—Pizarro defeated the Sapa Inca, Atahuallpa. Ambushing Atahuallpa and his army in the town square at Cajamarca, the Spaniards slaughtered thousands of Incas and captured their emperor.

Desperate for his freedom, Atahuallpa offered to fill a room—about 22 feet long and 17 feet wide—with gold and silver. His subjects faithfully supplied more than 11 tons of gold and 26,000 pounds of silver, worth hundreds of millions of dollars today, to ransom him. The Incas kept their side of the bargain. The Spaniards, however, took the treasure but executed Atahuallpa anyway.

Nor did the gold and silver given for Atahuallpa's ransom satisfy their greed. In 1533 conquistadors plundered the Inca capital, Cuzco. They tore down the gold walls of the city's Temple of the Sun and ransacked its tombs, searching for gold objects buried with the dead. Still not satisfied, they pillaged other parts of the empire, fired by rumors of more riches.

Spanish fortune hunter Francisco Pizarro.

The Incas believed gold to be the sweat of the sun god, Inti, and silver the tears of the moon goddess, Mama-Quilla. They used it to craft ceremonial objects. For the Spaniards, however, gold and silver meant only one thing: great wealth. They melted down exquisite vases, jewelry, and figurines to form ingots easily distributed among themselves. Countless treasures displaying Inca craft were therefore lost in the furnaces of the Spaniards.

of their Inca builders, the sanctuary's stone walls showed no lasting damage when finally freed of their jungle overgrowth, hundreds of years later.

THE LURE OF LEGEND

So completely was Machu Picchu lost to the outside world, French explorer Eugène de Sartiges in 1834 slashed his way along abandoned trails within a few miles of its ruins without suspecting their existence. In his 1875 account of his travels through the Urubamba Valley northwest of Cuzco, fellow Frenchman Charles Weiner mentioned hearing of ruins at a place called Machu Picchu. However, he was never able to find them. It would be another quarter of a century or so before Machu Picchu reemerged from its jungle cover.

That reemergence owed a great deal to the ambitions of a Yankee enthusiast of South American history. Yale University graduate Hiram Bingham III first encountered Inca ruins on a trip to Peru in 1909. These remnants of an ancient, storied civilization sparked his imagination.

In the 1800s Inca history had been so romanticized that adventurers from all over the world made their way to Peru. They were in search not of Machu Picchu (which they had never heard of) but of Vilcabamba, the legendary refuge of the Incas who mounted a final, spirited resistance against the Spanish conquistadors. With the defeat of the rebels in 1572, this jungle retreat also mysteriously vanished. In the nineteenth and early twentieth centuries, the prospect of discovering Vilcabamba offered the ambitious a fast track to fame. At that time, archaeologists and explorers who uncovered the secrets of lost civilizations were treated like celebrities.

After his first visit to Peru in 1909, Bingham caught the fever to find Vilcabamba, the elusive "Lost City of the Incas." Returning home, he inspired his classmates at a Yale reunion with his desire to explore Inca lands. Together they convinced the university to fund an expedition to the largely uncharted hills around Cuzco. The expedition would investigate the plant and animal life of the region and, in the process, track down the legendary "Lost City."

RUMOR OF RUINS

With Bingham at its head, the Yale Peruvian Expedition of 1911 included Harry Ward Foote, a naturalist, and Dr. William G. Erv-

THE AMBITIOUS HIRAM BINGHAM

Hiram Bingham III may have found the ruins of Machu Picchu unexpectedly, but he intended to win the fame that came his way as a result. Early in the twentieth century, explorers enjoyed the celebrity status of pop stars today. Eager for fame, Bingham in 1911 determined to explore still-uncharted lands in South America.

Explorers face uncertainty and even danger. But Bingham willingly accepted the risks. He had something to prove. In 1900 he had married Alfreida Mitchell, heir to the Tiffany jewelry fortune. Bingham wanted to be known for more than just marrying into a famous family.

Bingham's discovery of Machu Picchu succeeded in winning him fame. An entire issue of *National Geographic* featured his 1912 expedition to clear and excavate the site. His photographs of Machu Picchu, filling the magazine's pages, thrilled the public. To Bingham's great satisfaction, the era's most famous explorers welcomed him into their ranks.

Bingham took advantage of his fame to enter politics. Connecticut elected him lieutenant governor in 1923 and governor in 1925. Also in 1925 he ran for the U.S. Senate and won. He represented Connecticut in the Senate for the next eight years. Bingham's political career, it may be said, was built on the ruins of Machu Picchu.

ing, a physician and surgeon. The Peruvian government contributed an armed escort, Sergeant Carrasco, who was fluent in the native Quechua language. Sergeant Carrasco had orders to follow Bingham wherever he went.

In the summer of 1911, Bingham and his band arrived in Cuzco, where Bingham pored over resources in the city's library for clues to his quest. In mid-July, Bingham—together with Foote, Erving, and their Peruvian escort—left Cuzco to explore the hills north of the city. Bingham was brimming with confidence. According to historian John Hemming:

Hiram Bingham had all the necessary qualities for finding Inca ruins: he was full of enthusiasm and curiosity, he was brave and tough, and he was something of a mountaineer and historian. He was also phenomenally lucky. His expedition was the first to use a new trail blasted through the mighty granite gorges of the Urubamba below [the village of] Ollantaytambo. The trail was rough, cut with great effort by government engineers to provide an outlet for coca and other produce from plantations on the lower river, but it opened a stretch of river that had been bypassed by all previous conquistadors and travelers.[3]

A week into the expedition, on July 23, the party turned off the newly opened trail to camp on a beach bordering the Urubamba River. On their way to the campsite, they passed a grass-covered hut. The owner of the hut, named Melchior Arteaga, approached the group and demanded to know why, unlike respectable travelers, they had avoided his "inn." Sergeant Carrasco managed to reassure Arteaga that the expeditionary team, being accustomed to camping out in the open, meant no offense. Carrasco explained that, with the approval of the Peruvian government, Bingham was searching for Inca ruins. Arteaga responded that he knew of some excellent ruins high atop a mountain called Huayna Picchu, rising above the opposite bank, and also on a nearby ridge known as Machu Picchu.

Arteaga agreed to guide Bingham to the ruins—for a fee. Bingham had less success persuading Foote and Erving to join him. Foote, the naturalist, said he expected to find more butterflies for study near the river. The surgeon had clothes to wash and mend. "No one supposed that [the ruins] would be particularly interesting," Bingham later wrote. "Anyhow it was my job to investigate all reports of ruins."[4] Only the duty-bound Sergeant Carrasco ended up accompanying Bingham. At ten o'clock on the drizzly morning of July 24, the two set off with Arteaga as a guide.

Arteaga led them a distance upstream, where a bridge crossed the rapids. The "bridge" consisted of half a dozen logs, some lashed together with vines. Rain had fallen the night before, swelling the river until it threatened to wash away the fragile crossing. Anyone unfortunate enough to fall into the rapids would succumb to the Urubamba's icy waters—if not first being dashed against sharp, jutting rocks. "I am frank to confess," Bingham wrote, "that I got down on my knees and crawled across, six inches at a time."[5]

Once across the bridge, Bingham and his companions struggled through thick jungle. They then climbed up a steep slope, sometimes holding on by their fingernails. Adding to the arduousness of the climb was the extreme humidity that day. The three men also faced the danger of poisonous snakes common to the area.

A GLIMPSE OF ANCIENT WALLS

Managing to escape harm, the weary band arrived just after noon at a hut perched two thousand feet or so above the river. A couple of Peruvians greeted them and gave them cool water from a nearby stream to drink. They also offered their guests a meal of cooked sweet potatoes.

The Peruvians, named Richarte and Alvarez, said they had found terraces nearby for raising crops. Hundreds of years before, the Incas had built the terraces to create plots of level farmland in this mountainous region. Richarte and Alvarez had salvaged the terraces from the jungle and in them grew potatoes and maize (a kind of corn), as well as beans, peppers, and sugarcane.

After their meal and a brief rest, Bingham and the faithful Carrasco resumed their trek to the ruins. Arteaga preferred to stay behind and gossip with Richarte and Alvarez. A young boy was sent along as a guide. Dedicated as he was to his mission, Bingham recalled he had only "the slightest expectation of finding anything more interesting than the ruins of two or three stone houses such as we had encountered at various places on the [newly opened government] road."[6]

Bingham's expectations rose, however, after rounding a promontory and mounting a series of stone-supported terraces. The terraces were marvelously constructed, each measuring ten feet high and hundreds of feet long. Following his young guide into the jungle beyond, Bingham suddenly found himself standing before "a maze of ancient walls."[7] Even hidden by bamboo thickets and tangled vines, the walls were clearly of fine quality.

"Owing to the absence of mortar," Bingham noted, "there were no ugly spaces between the rocks. They might have grown together."[8] So precise was the stonework Bingham saw at the site, no invading vine or bramble had been able to force its way in between individual blocks. "The superior character of the stone work," he concluded, "the presence of these splendid

The superb stonework of Machu Picchu, like the stone wall shown here, greatly impressed Hiram Bingham.

edifices, and of what appeared to be an unusually large number of finely constructed stone dwellings, led me to believe that Machu Picchu might prove to be the largest and most important ruin discovered in South America since the days of the Spanish conquest."[9]

CLEARING AWAY THE YEARS

Bingham knew he would need to offer evidence of his great find. "Fortunately," he wrote, "I had a good camera and the sun was shining."[10] Not that picture taking at the site was easy. Bingham more than once had to balance his tripod on the tip of a building's triangle-shaped gable, or roof peak, to get a shot.

But Bingham required more proof than a handful of photos. The ruins needed to be cleared and excavated before convincing the world of their importance. On returning to the United States, Bingham persuaded the National Geographic Society to grant him $10,000 for a second expedition. Yale University matched this amount, and in May 1912 Bingham left again for Peru.

Bingham assigned Kenneth C. Heald, a topographer, or surveyor and mapmaker, the task of opening up a new route to Machu Picchu. Porters would be carrying supplies to the site and, if all went as hoped, plenty of specimens out from it. However, the trail Arteaga led Bingham on was too hazardous for a team loaded with sixty pounds of baggage each on their backs. In addition, the makeshift bridge Bingham had crawled over on his initial visit to Machu Picchu had washed away. Heald and his crew, therefore, needed to construct a new crossing as well as a new trail up to the ruins.

Once Heald completed the route, the probing of Machu Picchu's secrets could begin. Dr. George F. Eaton and Elwood C. Erdis arrived at the site. Eaton, a bone specialist, would help identify any remains found among the ruins. Erdis, a civil engineer, would guide the search for artifacts.

But first, Erdis supervised the task of clearing the site. It took native workers four months to chop away gnarled thickets and vines from the ruins. In places, giant trees perched atop the gable ends of dwellings. "It was not the least difficult part of our work to cut down and get such trees out of the way without seriously damaging the house walls,"[11] Bingham noted. Amazingly, the walls had survived the crushing grip of the trees' roots.

Along with chopping down trees and shrubs and burning the resulting rubbish, workers busied themselves rubbing graffiti off the buildings' stone walls. Generations of Peruvians, stumbling upon the site, had scrawled their names in charcoal on the ruins. Moss had to be cleaned from the walls, too.

DIGGING FOR CLUES

Once the site was cleared, excavation could begin. It was hoped that excavating, or digging up, the area would reveal clues about its past inhabitants and their way of life. In one building workers dug to a depth of eight or nine feet, yet their efforts uncovered nothing. After a week only fragments of pottery had been found, underneath one of the terraces at the site.

Most of the structures to be excavated lay in the saddlelike ridge between the peaks of Machu Picchu and Huayna Picchu. However, Arteaga had told Bingham there were ruins atop Huayna Picchu itself. Assistant topographer Heald agreed to scout out these ruins. His journey up the cone-shaped mountain, related in the 1913 issue of *National Geographic* magazine, proved a harrowing one:

> I pushed on up the hill, clearing my way with the machete, or down on all fours, following a bear trail (of which

MUMMIES

The sixteenth-century chronicler Garcilaso de la Vega—known as El Inca because his mother was an Inca princess—recalled seeing royal mummies when he was a boy in Cuzco. During festivals, the mummies, dressed in gorgeous clothes, were paraded onto the main square. Garcilaso de la Vega managed to touch a mummy's finger. "It was hard and rigid like that of a wooden statue," he wrote in his *Royal Commentaries of the Incas*, as quoted in John Hemming's book *Machu Picchu.*

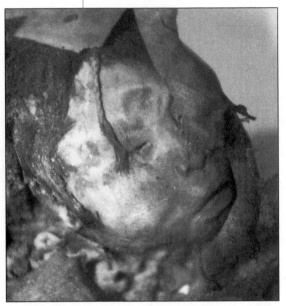
A five-hundred-year-old Inca mummy discovered in northern Argentina.

Garcilaso de la Vega guessed that a material like tar protected the mummies' leathery skin. The Incas' embalming secrets, however, remain unknown. Scholars do agree that the Incas dried the bodies of their dead naturally, exposing them in turn to night frosts and the sun at full strength to help preserve them. Knees were drawn up to the chin, making the resulting mummy bundle as compact as possible. Several layers of cloth swathed the body.

there were many). . . . The brush through which I made my way was in great part mesquite, terribly tough and with heavy, strong thorns. If a branch was not cut through at one blow, it was pretty sure to come whipping back and drive half a dozen spikes into hands, arms, and body. . . .

Finally, about 3 P.M., I had almost gained the top of the lowest part of the ridge, which runs along like the back-plates of some spined dinosaur. . . .

I was just climbing out on the top of the lowest "back-plate" when the grass and soil under my feet let go, and I dropped. For about 20 feet there was a slope of about 70 degrees, and then a jump of about 200 feet, after which it would be bump and repeat to the river.[12]

The tightly wound fabric continued to draw off fluids, keeping the body dry.

The Incas and other Andean peoples preserved the bodies of the deceased because they believed that their life force persisted after death. The dead were even offered food and drink. (The food was burned sacrificially in a brass pot and the drink poured into a basin.) To appear more lifelike to its human caretakers, a mummy bundle was often fitted with a false head topped by a wig and headdress.

The Incas believed that attentiveness to the dead helped ensure their goodwill. A fruitful harvest depended on the benevolence of ancestors. The Incas also believed that mummies delivered messages to the living, through interpreters. In addition, mummies possessed healing powers. Mummies of royalty in particular were revered as sacred objects.

Mummy bundles were not buried in the ground in the European way, but instead placed in niches carved in shrines or in caves. Efforts by the Spaniards to impose Christian burial on the Incas at first met with resistance. Believing the dead suffered under the weight of the earth, the Incas secretly dug up the bodies and placed them in traditional burial sites. Only when the Spanish priests convinced them that, wandering without graves, the souls of the dead took revenge on the living did the Incas accept Christian burial practices.

Fortunately, Heald managed to grab hold of a mesquite bush growing about five feet above the jump-off. The speed of his downward slide so jerked his grasping arm that ligaments were torn. But Heald survived. Five days later he bravely attempted the climb again. Not until the third try did he reach the summit of Huayna Picchu. There he discovered stone flights of stairs leading to expertly constructed walls, niches, and doorways.

Patience and perseverance were also needed to explore Machu Picchu's burial sites, which promised a wealth of skeletons for study. But most of the burial caves dotted the mountainsides below the ruins, making them difficult to find. The Incas purposely placed their dead in inaccessible places to discourage robbers from plundering the precious objects buried with the corpses, as well as predatory animals from disturbing the remains. Steep, rocky slopes, as well as the surrounding thorny scrub and plentiful snake population, made reaching the caves a daunting task.

Following two days' search by natives hired by Bingham's expedition team, not a single burial cave was found. Bingham suspected that the natives feared a curse on their crops if they disturbed the sacred resting places of their Andean ancestors. To help overcome such fears, Bingham offered a reward of a Peruvian silver dollar to anyone who located a cave harboring a skull. "No possible amount of agricultural good luck," Bingham wrote, "could compete with such a bonus as we had offered."[13] The next day eight burial caves were reported found by the native crew.

A LASTING LEGACY

Eventually, more than a hundred graves in the vicinity of Machu Picchu were excavated. These excavations produced partial as well as complete skeletons. Bingham estimated that the expedition unearthed a total of 173 individuals.

Artifacts such as this three-legged brazier (left) and two-handled water jar (right) have been unearthed at Machu Picchu.

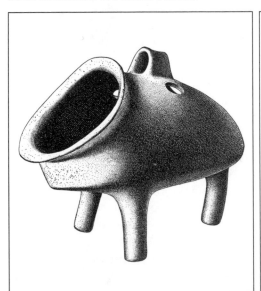

Burial caves at Machu Picchu also produced remnants of pottery and other artifacts. Women were usually buried with their blackened cooking pots, as well as with their sewing needles, made from plant spines, and tools of sharpened animal bone used in hand looms. Construction tools including bronze axes, chisels, and crowbars were often found alongside skeletons identified as males. Polishing and grinding stones, also used by Inca construction workers, appeared in burial caves as well. Ornaments buried with their owners included bronze shawl pins. One pin was cunningly carved to resemble the head of a hummingbird, complete with a long, curved beak.

But whatever artifacts that excavation crews found at Machu Picchu, the greatest discovery made by Bingham and his team remains the site itself. Clearing Machu Picchu of its jungle cover revealed its magnificence to the world. The skill of Inca builders could be seen not only in the beauty of Machu Picchu, but also in the solidity of its construction. The site withstood destruction by earthquakes and landslides, which menaced the region. It also prevailed against the erosive forces of wind and water. As Bingham predicted, Machu Picchu has become the most famous archaeological site in South America. It also remains one of the most mysterious.

A Puzzling Purpose

The purpose of Machu Picchu is another one of its mysteries. Because the Incas left no written records and the Spanish chroniclers failed to mention the site, there has been much speculation about why Machu Picchu was built and the part it played in Inca life and culture.

Speculation about Machu Picchu began when it was first recovered from its jungle overgrowth. Hiram Bingham was quick to propose his own theories about Machu Picchu. Bingham mistakenly believed that in Machu Picchu he had discovered a legendary lost city.

A Legendary Site

When Bingham first stumbled onto the ruins of Machu Picchu, he believed he had found the last bastion of Inca resistance against the Spanish invaders: the legendary city of Vilcabamba. "The royal city of [Vilcabamba] was completely lost," wrote Bingham. "It was a sacred shrine hidden on top of great precipices in a stupendous canyon where the secret of its existence was safely buried for three centuries under the shadow of Machu Picchu mountain."[14]

The evidence, however, argues against Bingham's claim that Machu Picchu was the fabled "Lost City of the Incas." First, the sixteenth-century chroniclers place Vilcabamba in a wide valley, while Machu Picchu sits on a high, narrow ridge. Second, the routes the Spanish reportedly traveled to Vilcabamba do not match those leading to Machu Picchu. Finally, a document written in 1572, of which Bingham was unaware, describes the roof of Vilcabamba's palace as tiled, in imitation of the Spanish style, instead of thatched in the usual Inca way. However, no roofing tiles have ever been unearthed at Machu Picchu.

Bingham did discover such tiles among the ruins in a place called Espíritu Pampa, meaning "Plain of Ghosts." In 1911, after catching his first glimpse of Machu Picchu, Bingham pressed on to the northwest. There, at Espíritu Pampa, he found ruins overgrown with jungle greenery. Most of the available evidence points to these ruins as the remains of Vilcabamba.

A Shelter for "Chosen Women"

Bingham proposed another theory about the purpose of Machu Picchu. He suggested that in the upheaval following the Spanish conquest, the site provided a refuge for *acllas*, or "chosen women." Selected at a young age, primarily for their beauty, *acllas* were devoted to serving the Incas' patron deity, the sun god, Inti—as well as the Inca ruler, known as the Sapa Inca, who was believed to be Inti's descendant on earth. The duties of *acllas* of the royal household included weaving exquisite cloth and preparing elaborate meals for the Sapa Inca. Additionally, they fed the Sapa Inca by hand and even held out their palms to catch his spit.

Bingham imagined the last Inca rulers living at Machu Picchu, pampered by *acllas*. After the Spanish defeated the Inca rebels, the *acllas* remained in hiding at Machu Picchu, according to Bingham. "Here, concealed in a canyon of remarkable grandeur, protected by nature and by the hand of man, the [*acllas*], one by one[,] passed away on this beautiful mountain top and left no descendants willing to reveal the importance or explain the significance of the ruins which crown the . . . precipices of Machu Picchu,"[15] he wrote.

As proof of his theory that Machu Picchu was a refuge for *acllas*, Bingham cited his team's excavation of burial caves at the site. The team claimed that 80 percent of the bones in these caves belonged to women. However, reexamination of the remains has determined that males and females are equally represented in Machu Picchu's burial sites, contradicting Bingham's theory.

A Mountain Citadel

Some have speculated that Machu Picchu was built as a citadel, or mountain fortress, guarding entry to the Inca capital, Cuzco,

The Sapa Inca (center) is flanked by an aclla (right) and a servant (left) in this undated painting.

less than thirty-five miles away. Just to the east threatened the fierce tribes of the Amazon rain forest. And to the west, across the Apurímac River, a federation of tribes, known as the Chanca, stood ready to attack the Inca Empire. Machu Picchu, then, may have served as a first line of defense against invaders bent on capturing Cuzco.

The site clearly provided natural defenses from unwanted visitors. On three sides, flanking the mountain saddle where Machu Picchu sits, sheer cliffs fall sharply to the rapids of the

"A LIFE OF TREMENDOUS PLEASURE AND AMUSEMENT"

A select group of women in Inca times, known as *acllas*, served as priestesses of the sun god, Inti, and as attendants of the semidivine Sapa Inca. Scouts of the Sapa Inca searched the empire for promising young candidates to join the ranks of these "chosen women." Selected at about the age of ten, candidates entered convents known as *acllahuasis*. Estimates are that at any given time, as many as fifteen thousand women and girls lived cloistered in *acllahuasis* throughout the empire.

The training of novice *acllas* prepared them for the role they would play in Inca society. Older priestesses of Inti, or *mamaconas*, taught them to perform such tasks as dyeing and weaving; preparing *chicha*, a beer made from maize (a type of corn), which the Incas indulged in at festivals and other ceremonies; and conducting religious rites. Weaving was a skill particularly valued by the Incas: The weaving of *cumba*—a fine wool whose threads included bat hair—into clothes for the Sapa Inca was a duty entrusted to the "chosen women."

After three years of training, novice *acllas* underwent a further selection process. The Sapa Inca chose some to join his household; others he married off to his nobles and other political allies to reward their loyal service. The remainder became Virgins of the Sun, symbolically married to Inti. As priestesses, they prepared sacrificial foods and presided over religious shrines and rituals.

Befitting their lofty position in Inca society, the Virgins of the Sun led a privileged life. The book *Incas: Lords of Gold and Glory* by the Editors of Time-Life Books quotes one Spanish chronicler's observation that these women "lived the life of great queens and ladies, and a life of tremendous pleasure and amusement, and they were very highly regarded, esteemed and loved." Few pleasures were denied them—an exception being the pleasure of a sexual relationship. A Virgin of the Sun was strictly bound by a vow of chastity. Breaking this vow meant death for both the man and the woman, and even for the man's family and members of his village.

A mamacona addresses a group of acllas *during an Inca ceremony.*

The hilltop garrison of Sacsahuaman (pictured) served as the primary military stronghold for the Inca capital city, Cuzco.

Urubamba River. A tributary of the mighty Amazon, the Urubamba is impassable due to high waters during at least half the year. On the fourth side of the site, originally the only access to the mountain of Machu Picchu, was a narrow trail dropping away to steep cliffs.

Most scholars, however, remain unconvinced that Machu Picchu was built to be a defensive post protecting the Inca heartland. Machu Picchu was militarily insignificant, they claim, compared with the fortifications of Sacsahuaman, an immense stronghold built on a hilltop overlooking Cuzco. Sacsahuaman boasts three towers as well as saw-toothed ramparts.

By contrast, Machu Picchu's dry moat and low enclosing walls appear to have served a symbolic rather than a practical purpose. That is, these features express the idea that Machu Picchu was a special place that not everyone could enter—only a select few were permitted to pass through its impressive main gate, the Intipunku, or Gate of the Sun. Such man-made barriers highlighted the site's natural isolation, though they fail to offer any convincing evidence that Machu Picchu served as a citadel.

A REMOTE SANCTUARY

It is most likely that Machu Picchu was some sort of sanctuary or shrine. Archaeological evidence supports this theory. Strung along a route now known as the Inca Trail, linking Machu Picchu with Cuzco to the southeast, lay clusters of ruins with such Quechua names as Huinay Huayna, Huayna Quente, and Phuyu Pata Marca. An expedition led by American archaeologist Paul Fejos in 1940 excavated these ruins. Fejos concluded that in Inca times each site represented a combination ceremonial site and way station, or rest stop. Although several of the ruins feature fountains and fine stonework, Machu Picchu is larger and more magnificent than any of them. Possibly, for the Incas, each served as a pilgrimage center where those destined for Machu Picchu performed purification rites before approaching the sacred site.

Today most scholars agree that Machu Picchu was a religious retreat reserved for Inca royalty. It was common for Inca

Agricultural terraces (background, left) and communal living quarters (center) lay at the base of Machu Picchu's eastern peaks.

royalty to build estates in the scenic countryside north of Cuzco, where they found refuge from the capital city. Such estates operated as self-sufficient communities, with their own living quarters, agricultural facilities, and shrines. In these country villas, the Sapa Inca could carry out his duties away from the clamor of the capital. In the shadow of Machu Picchu's sacred peaks, the Sapa Inca is imagined to have engaged in ceremonies and rituals appropriate to his role as spiritual leader as well as head of state.

The abundance of fine architecture at Machu Picchu also indicates it may have been some sort of elite sanctuary. The remarkable stonework displayed in its buildings, along with its elegantly built agricultural terraces and elaborate waterworks, shows a huge investment of labor. Such intensive commitment of resources distinguishes Inca royal retreats from other settlements in the empire. Furthermore, the large number of splendid buildings at Machu Picchu suggests that its inhabitants were predominately upper class.

A PROJECT OF PACHACUTI

It is now widely believed that Machu Picchu was built as a retreat at the command of the Inca ruler known as Pachacuti and then maintained after his death by his *panaqa*. The royal *panaqa* consisted of the descendants of the Sapa Inca other than his successor. "When the king died," explained Spanish chronicler Bernabé Cobo, "the prince did not inherit his palace and fortune: it was left, together with the body of the deceased, to the clan he had founded. The entire estate was dedicated to the cult of his body and the support of his family."[16] Dead emperors therefore continued to preside over their property through their *panaqas*.

Beginning in 1438, Pachacuti embarked on a series of conquests resulting in the vast Inca Empire. Before his wars of expansion ended, the Incas, once an undistinguished Andean tribe, had evolved into an imperial power. Cobo wrote that Pachacuti's conquests included the upper reaches of the Urubamba River valley, which include the site of Machu Picchu—an area Cobo described as "a difficult country to subdue because of its wildness and extensive undergrowth and dense jungles."[17]

Pachacuti understood that, ultimately, empire building took place beyond the battlefield. So he undertook ambitious

"HE WHO SHAKES THE EARTH"

The Inca ruler known as Pachacuti is credited with building the largest empire in the Americas before the coming of Columbus. John Hemming, in his book *Machu Picchu*, calls Pachacuti "the Napoleon of the Incas, a successful conqueror who had the energy to supervise every detail of the administration of his empire."

As a young man, Pachacuti was known as Yupanqui, a prince of the Incas, one among many tribes inhabiting the Andean region. In 1438 the Incas were attacked by the Chanca, a power-hungry federation of tribes who swept down from the west, intent on devouring Inca lands. The Inca ruler, Viracocha, responded to the crisis by fleeing the capital city, Cuzco, with his heir, Prince Urco. Viracocha's younger son, Yupanqui, took up the seemingly lost cause of defending the city. Against all odds, he succeeded. So miraculous was the Incas' victory, legend says the stones on the battlefield turned into warriors to fight alongside them.

Threatened by Yupanqui's rising popularity, Viracocha ordered Urco to slay his brother, but Urco lost his own life in the attempt. Disgraced, Viracocha was forced to give up his rule to Yupanqui.

Yupanqui decreed that he would now be called Pachacuti, meaning "he who shakes the earth" in the Quechua language. He then proceeded to live up to the name. The Andean region underwent a revolution under his leadership. A series of conquests multiplied the territory under his control, while his reorganization of society enlarged the scope of his authority. He expanded not only Inca lands, but also the code of laws and religious practices governing his people's lives. The spiritual as well as political head of the empire, he orchestrated many of the ceremonies that, along with his armies, held the people he conquered in thrall. The ambitious building projects he initiated—including monuments like Machu Picchu— were designed to display his power and command as well as consolidate his far-flung empire.

construction projects to solidify his conquests—and glorify his rule. Very possibly Pachacuti built Machu Picchu to symbolize his dominance over the Urubamba region, which he now controlled and which he could view from Machu Picchu's commanding heights.

Evidence supporting Pachacuti as the person behind its construction recently came to light. In the library of a Cuzco monastery, scholars Luis Miguel Glave, María Remy, and John Rowe found a document from 1568 that mentions an estate belonging to the *panaqa* of Pachacuti at "Picho," north of the capital city. "It would be apt that he, the greatest Inca," writes photojournalist Max Milligan, "should have had Machu Picchu constructed as a sacred retreat."[18]

By constructing Machu Picchu out of the sacred rock of the Andes mountains, Pachacuti showed his godlike ability to reshape the landscape. The setting for Machu Picchu was apparently chosen for its proximity to natural objects the Incas considered holy. There, in their midst, Pachacuti ordered a magnificent sanctuary built to rival their own stunning beauty.

HUACAS AT MACHU PICCHU

Machu Picchu's setting was full of religious significance for the Incas. The Inca religion was animistic, meaning the Incas believed that natural objects, on earth and in the skies, were inhabited by spiritual energies. These spirit-dwelling objects, called *huacas*, inspired the Inca's worship.

Rivers, mountain peaks, constellations of stars—all powerful *huacas*—encircle Machu Picchu. From its mountain perch, the site looks down more than fifteen hundred feet to the churning waters of the Urubamba River—a *huaca* often called the Celestial River by the people of the Andes, who believed it mirrored the Milky Way. In addition, the mountain peaks cradling the site—Machu Picchu to the south and Huayna Picchu to the north, as well as the rounded peak of Putucusi rising across the river—were revered by Andean tribes, including the Incas. Also considered sacred, the glacier-topped Mount Salcantay twelve miles distant is visible from the summit of Huayna Picchu. On Huayna Picchu's north slope, Machu Picchu's builders constructed a cavelike shrine facing the Pleiades, a cluster of stars worshiped by the Incas.

Huacas not only encircle Machu Picchu; they also exist within the site itself. Boulders and outcrops, or masses, of rock were among the natural objects the Incas believed to be sacred. The planners of Machu Picchu intentionally incorporated the huge masses of rock into their architecture. The Incas were certainly able to remove these features of the landscape if they chose to. Yet they not only worked stone outcrops into their building plan, they also built structures to accommodate them. Anthropologist Margaret Greenup MacLean explains: "Carved or uncarved, these boulders were crucial elements in the animistic Inca religious philosophy. Therefore, they have to have been a strong consideration in the spatial organization of the site."[19]

A rounded wall surrounds a sacred granite boulder in the Inca sun temple high above the Urubamba River valley.

A SOLAR OBSERVATORY

Probably the most striking example at Machu Picchu of construction to accommodate a sacred rock is the building complex identified as a temple to the sun. Some have even speculated that Machu Picchu may have been one big solar observatory; they note that Machu Picchu's location, high in the Andes, made it an excellent place for keeping an eye on the sun's movements. A curved wall of Machu Picchu's supposed sun temple surrounds a mighty granite boulder. A cut edge of the boulder points toward a window framing the area of the sky where the sun rises at the winter solstice. The

The Intihuatana monolith was used during Inca sun worship at Machu Picchu. The altar is carved from a single piece of granite.

solstice marks Earth's farthest distance from the sun in its orbit around the star—a period of anxiety for the Incas, who believed they derived their existence from the sun. It is thought that at dawn on the winter solstice (June 21 in the Southern Hemisphere), the sun would shine through the window of the temple, highlighting the sacred rock inside. Thus, when the sun traveled its farthest from Earth, the Incas would symbolically keep it close and so triumph over cold and hunger for yet another year.

Some propose that the Incas also attempted to hinder the sun's flight at Machu Picchu with a ritual at the stone altar known as the Intihuatana. Intihuatana is most often translated as "Hitching [tying] Post of the Sun." This translation reflects the belief that here Inca priests performed a ritual aimed at tying the sun to the altar and so preventing its early departure at the winter solstice. "It is probable that the priests of the Sun, whose lives depended on their being successful in appearing to control [the Inca sun god Inti's] actions, had learned to read the length of the shadows cast by the huge sundials called *intihuatana*, or, 'the place to which the sun is tied,'"[20] Bingham noted.

The Incas' agricultural, as well as religious, calendar required the close monitoring of Inti as he journeyed across the sky. According to chronicler Felipé Guamán Poma de Ayala:

They calculated the month, day, hour and precise moment for sowing their crops, observing the movements of the sun. They observed the way in which its rays illuminated the highest peaks in the mornings and how they penetrated the windows of their houses. Variations in its direction and intensity acted as a precise clock to regulate the sowing and harvesting of their foods.[21]

AN INTIMATE KNOWLEDGE OF NATURE

Other speculations about Machu Picchu have been popularized by New Age thinking, which claims great respect for the traditions of native, or indigenous, peoples such as the Incas. New Agers believe that indigenous cultures experience a very close

THE ANDES

Machu Picchu owes its spectacular views to its mountain setting. The Andes soar above every other mountain range except the Himalayas, located in Asia. Many of the Andes' peaks are more than twenty thousand feet high. And because the mountain range is a geologically young system, it continues to rise.

Formed millions of years ago from a collision of the earth's shifting crustal plates, the Andes remain susceptible to violent geologic forces. Earthquakes rock the area, and volcanic eruptions continue to transform the landscape. Adding to the forbidding quality of the region, mountain passes are tortuously narrow and dizzyingly steep. Most lie more than three thousand meters above sea level.

Stretching nearly five hundred miles—the length of the entire western coast of South America—the Andes wind through six more countries. Indeed, the Andes form the longest mountain range in the world above sea level. Defying the risks, people have inhabited the high plateaus and mountain valleys of the Andes for thousands of years. Machu Picchu rests on the eastern slope of the range, in present-day Peru.

The sedimentary rock of the Andes contains a wealth of copper. Evidently the name Andes comes from the native Quechua word for "copper": *anti*. Significantly, copper was the hardest metal used by the Incas.

connection to the natural world. Native cultures, for example, traditionally seek to maintain harmony among all things in the universe.

According to New Age interpretation, indigenous peoples link physical features on the earth around them with objects in the sky above them. "The forces that exist beyond the earth, such as . . . the Sun, the Moon and the Stars have limited power until they are represented on the earth as landmarks," explains New Age proponent Val Jon Farris. Farris claims that Machu Picchu is such a landmark. He adds that the Incas modeled Machu Picchu after the mythical Llulli, an enormous bird with iridescent wings, sent by the sun god, Inti, to restore harmony when human society dissolves into chaos and whose presence "evokes reverence and peace."[22] Presumably, so does its earthly representation: Machu Picchu.

New Agers also honor Machu Picchu as a totemic spot or vortex, that is, a place where powerful forces flowing through the universe concentrate. "It is in that place," Farris writes, "all the magical and mysterious forces of the earth and sky [come together]."[23] To pay homage to these forces, and to draw on their power, followers of New Age beliefs hold spiritual ceremonies at Machu Picchu.

According to New Age devotees, the Incas' intimacy with nature explains their skillful manipulation of natural materials—for example, their incorporation of massive stones into buildings at Machu Picchu without the use of wheeled devices or iron tools. But whether or not the achievement of Machu Picchu can be attributed to an indigenous people's spiritual connection with ancient, primal forces, it is clear that the Incas took full advantage of available resources to create this enduring monument to their civilization.

LAYING THE
GROUNDWORK

Once the remote mountain setting of Machu Picchu was selected, building could begin. Building required a plan and also a
supply of tools and labor. In addition, the site needed to be
cleared and prepared to support the proposed sanctuary. An infrastructure had to be provided, meaning water and drainage
systems had to be established, along with roads and bridges
linking Machu Picchu with the rest of the Inca Empire. With an
infrastructure in place, Machu Picchu's buildings and inhabitants could better survive natural disasters common to the region, such as earthquakes and landslides.

A MODEL DESIGN

Because no written records about Machu Picchu exist, historians
can only speculate how plans for it developed and were carried
out. Evidence does exist, however, that Inca architects used
models to aid in the planning process. These models displayed
the architects' designs in miniature. Such three-dimensional
representations offered Inca architects a way to communicate
their ideas without use of pen and paper.

Chronicler Garcilaso de la Vega recalled seeing a model of
the Inca capital city, Cuzco:

> I saw the model of Cuzco and part of the surrounding
> areas in clay, pebbles, and sticks. It was done to scale
> with the squares, large and small; the districts and
> houses, even the most obscure; and the three streams
> that flow through the city, marvelously executed. The
> countryside with high hills and low flats and ravines,

rivers and streams with their twists and turns were all wonderfully rendered, and the best cosmographer [maker of three-dimensional maps] in the world could not have done it better.[24]

Chances are that a similar model of Machu Picchu was crafted—and approved by Sapa Inca Pachacuti, whose command drove the project—before construction began at the site. The effort that went into constructing Machu Picchu, seen in the fine quality of its buildings, would have demanded as much.

A MIRROR IMAGE?

There is evidence that Machu Picchu, like other Inca settlements, was carefully planned. Photographs of Inca sites taken from airplanes, for example, show that "established ideas were used, in part because of [the sites'] intricacy and . . . varying geometric designs,"[25] notes scholar John Hyslop. Details of Machu Picchu's design, however, are a matter of debate. Lack of architectural plans, blueprints, or maps prevent any satisfactory settlement of the debate.

Cuzco's Temple of the Sun incorporates the four-sided design that is commonly seen in Inca construction.

One theory claims that Machu Picchu's eastern and western sectors mirror each other. This theory was championed by Manuel Chávez Ballón, for many years custodian of the ruins. According to Ballón, each sector has its royal residence, temples, barracks for soldiers, storage facilities, and other fixtures of Inca planned cities.

Those who discount a mirror-image design for Machu Picchu point to its oblong plaza, which follows the irregular contours of the mountain terrain. If Machu Picchu had been designed strictly with a balanced, symmetrical layout in mind, it would instead feature a quadrilateral, or four-sided, plaza. Standard in population centers throughout Inca lands, the four-sided plaza symbolized the four quarters of the empire. Such a design scheme—meant to imitate Cuzco, the hub of the Inca Empire—gave conquered peoples an object lesson in how an ideal Inca community was organized.

Departures from this norm were common in royal estates and sanctuaries, which could not properly be called cities. Their populations were too small and select, housing mainly the Inca elite. In addition, they were built in settings chosen for their scenic beauty, whose rugged landscapes demanded a more improvised architectural design. As a retreat tucked away in the mountains, Machu Picchu probably followed a design custom-made for its unique setting.

PRIMITIVE TOOLS

However they debate the specifics of Machu Picchu's design, scholars agree the sanctuary was built using relatively unsophisticated tools. Fortunately, the stone available locally is full of fault lines, or cracks. For Machu Picchu's construction crew, such naturally occurring cracks significantly eased the task of prying away blocks of building stone from the bedrock, a process known as quarrying. Generally, workers fed cobbles—smooth, egg-shaped stones weighing anywhere from less than two to more than twenty pounds—into the cracks. They then repeatedly hammered at the cobbles to widen the cracks and eventually split the rock, making it easier to remove. Solid and compact, these cobbles were gathered from nearby streams. Known as *hihuana*, they were also used to shape the quarried blocks to ready them for building. "They had no other tools to work the stones than some black *hihuana*, with which they

Bronze tools like this knife (left) and axe (right) were used by the Incas to clear away thick jungle overgrowth during the construction of Machu Picchu.

dress [shape the stone] by pounding rather than cutting,"[26] noted chronicler Garcilaso de la Vega.

In the 1980s architect Jean-Pierre Protzen demonstrated the possibility of forming a ready-to-use building stone from a freshly quarried rock relying only on cobbles as tools. Working in an old Inca quarry about twenty miles from Cuzco, he first hammered a chunk of rock into a rough rectangle using one of the heavier cobbles on hand. Then, with smaller cobbles, he smoothed the sides of the rock and squared off its edges. Surprisingly, the job required less effort than Protzen had anticipated.

The Incas were forced to make do with a limited selection of tools because they never developed the ability to produce iron. "They did not know how to make anvils of iron" or "extract iron," or to "make hammers with wooden handles" or "tongs for removing the metal from the fire,"[27] wrote Garcilaso de la Vega. The strongest metal the Incas used was bronze, which they produced by combining copper and tin. Workers evidently used bronze crowbars, called *champis*, at Machu Picchu to help free blocks of stone from the quarry site. Such tools were discovered in burial caves near the ruins.

Not only did construction crews at Machu Picchu lack powerful iron tools to quarry stone but also to clear the area of thick jungle growth before building could begin. Axes were generally made of bronze, while knives, also used for clearing, were carved from obsidian or other hard stone. Equipped with these relatively primitive tools, laborers faced the backbreaking task of cutting back the tangled mass of vines and shrubs carpeting the area.

A LABOR FORCE

A large supply of workers was needed to complete such an ambitious project as Machu Picchu. The less sophisticated the technology, the greater the number of laborers required at a construction site. "A lack of tools or clever devices necessarily increases the volume of labor," wrote Spanish chronicler Bernabé Cobo, "and the [Incas] had to do it all by brute force."[28]

A huge workforce to do the empire's business was made possible by the Inca's tax system. Throughout Inca territory, households were subject to a tax payable in labor. This labor, re- ferred to as *mit'a*, might involve serving in the army, toiling in mines, or working on state building projects, including Machu Picchu. Any able-bodied man from eighteen to fifty years of age might be drafted for a period of *mit'a* service.

The Incas' forced labor system allowed the state to mobilize thousands of workers to Machu Picchu. Laboring in shifts, these workers could toil uninterruptedly. They could also be easily re- placed from the ranks of men throughout the empire eligible for the *mit'a*.

The building of Machu Picchu likely benefited from the readiness with which killed and injured workers could be re- placed. Casualties were probably common among construction crews at the site. Near-vertical cliffs and slippery soils risked the lives of *mit'a* laborers. Pointing out a stone platform built atop the peak of Machu Picchu, Hiram Bingham wrote:

> If any of the workmen who built this retaining [support- ing] wall on the very edge of the signal station slipped he must have fallen three thousand feet before striking any portion of the cliff broad enough to stop his body. I do not mind admitting that when I took pictures from it I not only lay flat on my stomach, I had two trusty Indians hang on to my legs. It really was a dizzy height. But imagine building a wall on it![29]

The mountainous site not only endangered workers with slips and falls. Less oxygen reaches the lungs at higher altitudes, resulting in a condition called altitude sickness. Until the body adapts, headaches, coughing, nausea, as well as difficulty breathing can result. The exertion demanded by physical labor would have worsened these symptoms for newly arrived *mit'a* crews. While chewing the leaf of the coca plant somehow relieves the damaging effects of altitude sickness, this remedy was denied to common laborers. Only the Inca elite had access to the potent plant.

Terrace walls ranging from five to thirteen feet in height stabilize a hillside residence.

TERRACING

While it risked the lives of laborers, the construction of retaining walls on Machu Picchu's mountainsides was a necessary part of terracing. Terracing involves compacting earth fill behind sturdy retaining walls. The Incas used terracing to level mountain terrain and so prepare it for building. Building on relatively level ground produces more durable structures than building on slopes. Terracing also stabilizes slopes against the threat of landslides. In addition, terracing allowed the Incas to farm the steep, stony land of the Andes.

Andean peoples had been taming the terrain with terraces for many centuries, but the Incas perfected the technique. Inca terraces ranged between five and thirteen feet, and their walls sloped back slightly to help support the weight of the earth behind them. Atop this earth fill, a layer of rich topsoil generally 1½ feet thick was hand-placed by *mit'a* laborers to form an agricultural terrace. The soil had been carried up from surrounding valleys in baskets strapped to workers' backs.

Retaining walls of terraces were built using either rough fieldstones or finely shaped boulders called ashlars. The fieldstone type closely followed the natural contours of the terrain. The ashlar type, however, molded slopes into elegant curves and zigzags and even straight lines.

These more elaborately constructed terraces predominate at Machu Picchu. Possibly the finely formed terraces provided a stage for agricultural rituals performed by the Sapa Inca himself. Such rituals honored the growing cycles of crops, particularly maize.

LAYING FOUNDATIONS

To help stabilize the retaining walls of terraces as well as the walls forming their buildings, the Incas built sturdy foundations underlying them. Such foundations root Machu Picchu's buildings firmly underground. Following their inspection of the site, engineering consultant Kenneth R. Wright and archaeologist Alfredo Valencia Zegarra concluded, "One may say the miracle of Machu Picchu is not only its beautiful buildings, but also the . . . features that lie unseen beneath the ground, where an estimated 60 percent of the Inca construction effort centered."[30]

Considerable effort went into establishing a sturdy foundation. To create a firm bedding for the foundation, *mit'a* workers arranged rocks and gravel along the bottom of pits dug in the ground. Providing backfill for the pits, the rocks—particularly large ones—were placed to cover crevices, while the gravel was added to fill gaps and help ensure a uniform surface for the overlying foundation. Construction of the foundation itself began with placing base rocks over flat stones of the backfill.

Sometimes huge rocks at the building site were selected for the foundation base. Masons, or stoneworkers, shaped the rock to provide an even building surface.

PROVIDING SURFACE DRAINAGE

Along with extensive foundations, Wright and Zegarra's "unseen" Machu Picchu includes water-drainage technology. Techniques

A sophisticated water-drainage system diverts water away from wall foundations, preventing erosion and landslides.

derived from trial and error, and also transmitted from generation to generation, allowed Inca builders to design very effective drainage systems.

Water-drainage systems are critical to the safety of buildings and the people dwelling in them. Heavy rainfall not only causes flooding but also breaks up soils to the point that landslides endanger lives and property. Indeed, Machu Picchu's stormy climate and its steep, slide-prone slopes threatened to crumble its stone buildings, causing their collapse.

To avoid this danger, Inca builders provided for surface drainage throughout Machu Picchu's urban sector. Strategically placed wall-drainage outlets, as well as drainage channels, diverted water from around the sector's buildings and plazas. At the entrance to what was apparently the royal residence, workers built a drainage channel. This channel kept standing water from collecting into a bothersome puddle at the doorway.

Elsewhere in the urban sector, alongside a huge boulder known as the Sacred Rock, stand two buildings. During Inca times, water runoff from the southernmost building's roof threatened to seep into the foundation, weakening it. To prevent this damage, Inca masons carved a drip line into a large stone located behind the building. Rain then dripped off the roof of the building onto the stone, to be carried away by the groove carved into its surface.

A centralized main drain collected runoff from both the urban and agricultural sectors of Machu Picchu for release into the forest below. The Incas built this drain to run east-west between the sectors. During construction of agricultural terraces near the main drain, builders apparently encountered an earth slide. To stabilize the area, workers took steps to control surface water runoff. They constructed an interceptor surface drain running north-south, to pass through the main drain and increase overall drainage. Evidence of their success in correcting the slippage is a damage-free stairway running almost directly over the geologic fault causing the slide.

PROVIDING SUBSURFACE DRAINAGE

The Incas allowed for subsurface drainage as well. A subsurface-drainage system directs excess water deep underground, where it then flows as groundwater. The Incas created such a system in Machu Picchu's agricultural sector. If water is allowed to drench the soil so that it fails to drain properly, it threatens to rot the roots of crops planted in that soil; a drainage system permits air to enter the soil and so promotes crop health. To engineer subsurface drainage in their agricultural terraces, the Incas placed a layer of fine sand and gravel below the topsoil, and below that, a layer of medium gravel. The porous quality of this gravelly earth drew water below the surface. Water naturally trickled down to these deeper, permeable zones. In even deeper strata, Inca workers created water-flow paths with loosely packed rocks and sometimes stone chips recycled from stonecutting.

Similar drainage devices are found in Machu Picchu's urban area. Excavators have exposed a three-foot-deep subsurface layer of loose rock and chipped stone below the city's central plaza. Evidently this three-foot layer of fill collected rainwater

THE SACRED WATER CYCLE

Because rainfall is unpredictable in the Andes, mountain springs provide a vital water supply for Andean peoples. Man-made hydraulic, or water, systems that helped manage this supply were highly prized. Machu Picchu's hydraulic system brought water to the site, carried it through the sanctuary, and allowed it to drain into the river bordering its mountain perch. Clearly, much effort went into constructing the series of fountains at Machu Picchu, which conducted fresh springwater through the sanctuary.

The fine stonework on display in the fountains supports the theory that they provided a stage for ritual ceremonies. The Incas' rituals tied in closely with their myths, and water played a significant role in Inca mythology. The Incas saw the world as surrounded by water: The Milky Way was a great river coursing through the cosmos; reaching the earth as rainfall, its sacred waters were carried by mountain springs to lakes and rivers, to collect there until draining into a vast sea underneath the earth. Machu Picchu's waterworks symbolized this cosmic flow in their conduct of springwater from the heights of the mountains to the depths of the Urubamba.

A closer look at the fountains confirms their ceremonial purpose. Proceeding on from fountain to fountain, the water flowing through them would have dirtied too quickly for ordinary bathing and washing. Also, even when plugged, the drain holes were so far down the side, the basins could not have held much water. Instead, ablutions, or ceremonial washings, probably took place at Machu Picchu's cascade of fountains.

seeping below the surface. The rainwater then drained leisurely as groundwater.

The Incas apparently tapped into this groundwater, fed by their subsurface-drainage systems, to ensure Machu Picchu's water supply. On the lower east slope downhill from the sanctuary, several stone reservoirs have been discovered. These ancient water-collection tanks were built to intercept the flow of groundwater. Emptying into the reservoirs, the groundwater provided a secondary source of water for the residents of Machu Picchu. Their primary source was an assortment of mountain springs, whose fresh water was conducted to the sanctuary by means of a water-supply canal.

DRAWING ON NATURAL SPRINGS

Machu Picchu's water-supply canal was a conduit, or channel, built of stone. Evidence from an unfinished branch canal suggests that an experienced stonecutter built the two ends of the channel first. Less-skilled workers then connected the ends. Fieldstones formed the bottom and sides of the rectangular canal. These stones were flattened on the side lining the channel. The flattened stones created tight joints, which workers sealed with clay. This technique kept water seepage to a minimum. It is estimated that the canal could carry up to eighty gallons per minute.

Drawing on the power of gravity, the canal carried water down from the mountain of Machu Picchu to the heart of the sanctuary about a mile away. A year-round spring, serving as the site's chief water source, arose on the northern slope of Machu Picchu mountain.

Inca engineers cleverly increased the yield of this spring from what the water-supply canal could carry. They built a permeable stone wall about forty-eight feet long (about the distance of a fifth-floor window to the ground below) into Machu Picchu's north face. At the foot of the wall, they constructed a wide trench. Springwater then trickled through the stone wall to collect in the trench. These water-collection works were accessed by a terrace more than five feet wide, supported by a stone wall along the entire length of the collection area.

Also on the north slope of Machu Picchu, the Incas built a terrace to support the supply canal as it filled with water from the mountain springs. A series of stone-walled terraces continued to bolster the canal against slippage all along its route. After leaving the mountainside, the canal coursed through Machu Picchu's agricultural sector, branching off here and there to water crops. At one point, the canal spanned the main drain. Finally, through a groove in the inner city wall, the water-supply canal, and its contents, passed into urban Machu Picchu.

BRINGING FRESH WATER TO THE SITE

A series of sixteen fountains, stretching over a distance of 180 feet, brought the fresh springwater to the residents of Machu Picchu. Paralleling the fountains, a flight of 150 stone steps not only provided access to the fountains but also played a part in Machu Picchu's water system. Channels linking fountain to fountain ran underneath the stairway or, alternatively, alongside it. Also, if water ever threatened to flood the fountains, an outlet at the fourth fountain directed the overflow onto the stairway, where it spilled out over and down the steps.

All sixteen fountains in the series display fine masonry. They also all follow a basic design, though details differ. Besides a stone basin, generally carved from a single block of granite, each fountain has a back enclosing wall, a rectangular spout, and a round outlet, or drain. A narrow channel concentrated the

An outlet in Machu Picchu's subterranean water system allows for overflow should the channel become flooded.

flow of water at or near the top of the enclosing wall. Workers carefully shaped this channel into a kind of spout so the water poured into the basin below in a jet, or forceful stream. In some fountains, the stonecutters created a kind of lip on the spout to make sure the water jetted clear of the fountain's back wall. Keeping the jet clear of the wall helped preserve the stone from becoming eroded, or worn away, by the water.

At most 6 inches deep, the shallow basin catching the water stream measures about 18 inches wide, or about half the length of a yardstick. A hole, from 1½ to 2 inches in diameter, drilled in a corner of the basin drained water into the channel leading to the fountain below. The hole could be plugged, probably with a leaf, when it was necessary to fill the basin.

Such physical factors as gravity and the grade, or slope, of the water-supply canal determined the location of the first fountain in the series. The placement of this fountain, next to the royal residence, likely determined where the Inca architects located this very important building. Custom dictated that the Sapa Inca have first use of the fresh springwater.

In fact, establishing Machu Picchu's series of fountains probably marked the first phase of the urban sector's construction. Once the flow of precious water was assured through the heart of the sanctuary, building could proceed on the surrounding structures.

TRANSPORTING BUILDING BLOCKS

The spring on Machu Picchu's north slope serving as Machu Picchu's primary water source owed its existence in large part to the system of faults spread through the area. Spongy soil along one of the system's principal faults allowed the infiltration of rainwater, which bubbled to the surface in the form of a year-round spring.

The same fault system provided an ample supply of raw material for the builders of Machu Picchu. The faults produced an abundance of fractured rock, particularly granite, a durable building stone. Thanks to ancient landslides and rockfalls, an on-site quarry at Machu Picchu contained various sizes of white- to gray-colored granite blocks.

These mighty blocks had to be moved from the quarry, far to the site's southwest, to a particular construction area. Teams of workers hauled the huge rocks using ropes. Sometimes small

RESTORING INCA CANALS

Over the years the stone canals that had irrigated the Andean highlands in Inca times deteriorated into heaps of rubble. After the Spanish conquistadors had driven the people of the Andes off the land in the seventeenth century and forced them to toil in gold and silver mines, the canals fell into disrepair, causing the land to lose the fertility it had enjoyed under Inca management.

By the twentieth century, the land's infertility was forcing more and more families to move to Peru's already overpopulated cities. There, crowded into slums, families drifted deeper into poverty. Then, in the 1970s, a British archaeologist named Ann Kendall was inspired to restore the Inca canals and so revive agriculture in the rural districts outside Cuzco.

Kendall's archaeological research led her to apply Inca technology to the reconstruction of the irrigation canals. That meant relying on local materials, like clay, sand, and stone, and forgoing such modern inventions as cement. "Traditional technology is greatly preferable when you are dealing . . . in areas where tremors are common," Kendall told journalist Sally Bowen in Bowen's report, "Bringing the Inca Canals Back to Life," available on-line (at www.oneworld.org). "Clay is a far better sealant than cement and it remains damp and plastic. In an earthquake, cement cracks and falls apart, making for greater destruction. It works against the environment."

Kendall's first project was to restore a canal system for the village of Cusichaca, about seventy-five miles south of Machu Picchu. Under the direction of a master mason from Cuzco, members of the local community took up simple wood and stone tools like those used by their Inca ancestors and got to work.

The completion of the project, three years later, resulted in successful harvests of grains such as quinoa, as well as maize—an achievement that has revitalized the community. Farmers are not just feeding their families; they are profiting from the surplus sold in nearby markets. In addition, the population of Cusichaca is increasing, with families returning from as far away as Lima. Such success has been repeated elsewhere in the Urubamba Valley, promising renewed self-sufficiency to descendants of the Incas.

stones were placed underneath a particularly massive block to reduce the friction as the block dragged along the ground.

To lift the block into place on a building wall, the Incas maneuvered the block up a diagonal, or slanting, surface. Chronicler Bernabé Cobo wrote: "Having no cranes, wheels or lifting devices, they made a sloping ramp up against the building and lifted the stones by rolling them up this. As the building rose, they raised the ramp proportionately."[31] The ramp was formed of piled-up earth, over which wood beams were laid as rollers. The ramp was removed only after the stone was securely in place.

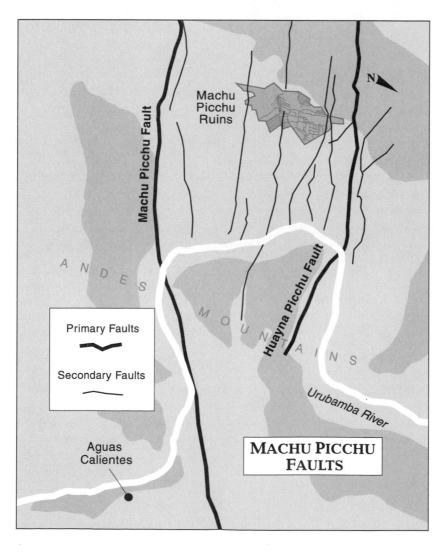

Several theories explain how Inca masons achieved the tight fit visible in their walls. One theory proposes that workers sprinkled fine sand over a row of boulders they had just placed. After positioning a stone in the row above, they hoisted it up again, possibly with a simple wooden lever. A mark was then left in the sand where the base layer needed to be pounded to accommodate the stone. Another theory suggests the stone was repeatedly positioned and raised to grind its surface and that of the base layer until they fit together snugly.

However it was accomplished, building stones often show indentations on their tops and bottoms. These hollowed-out areas helped embed ashlars, or shaped blocks, in stones above and below. A compact fit was the result.

These tight-fitting ashlars served a very practical purpose. Because two parallel faults border the site, buildings depending on mortar to bind stones together are liable to collapse in an earthquake. Yet when each block fits tightly against neighboring blocks, all the stones may shift against one another once the earth starts to pitch and roll, but they stay in place and ensure the building remains standing.

The buildings at the site are also protected against earthquake damage by walls that slant inward as they rise. This slope is repeated in the buildings' doors and windows. Inca masons followed this design to help stabilize their structures. Reducing the thrust bearing down on walls by widening their base helps keep them from collapsing.

"THE FINEST ROAD TO BE SEEN IN ALL THE WORLD"

Stones not only formed the bulk of buildings at Machu Picchu, they also were used to build the roads leading to and from the site. About ten thousand miles of stone-paved roadway connected the far-flung Inca Empire, including such remote mountain retreats as Machu Picchu. "[The Incas] built the finest road to be seen in all the world, and the longest, for it ran from Cuzco to Quito, and it joined another that led to Chile,"[32] wrote one Spanish chronicler. A weatherproof plaster made of corn leaves, pebbles, and clay covered some surfaces of the road. Low walls of stone prevented straying along certain stretches, while piles of rocks placed every sixty-six feet marked off distances on main routes.

Not only did the Inca road system speed the flow of communication and resources, including food and military personnel,

An Inca roadway descends the eastern slope of the Andes near the village of Taquesi in central Bolivia.

between the widespread parts of the empire, it also symbolized the empire's power and authority over its subjects. Forced *mit'a* labor built and maintained the road system. In fact, the average person would not have been allowed to use the roadway unless traveling with a *mit'a* labor team.

Travel on Inca roads was severely restricted. Guards checked that travelers were fulfilling some specific official duty. Among those permitted on the road were relay runners known as *chasqui.* On duty twenty-four hours a day, *chasqui* served fifteen-day rotations. They were entrusted with relaying verbal messages as well as bundles of *quipus* to and from Cuzco. A reinforcement relieved a runner every few miles, so that no time was lost in performing the Sapa Inca's business. The reinforcement ran alongside the runner long enough to hear a message or be passed a *quipu* bundle. So efficient was the *chasqui* system, the royal court at Cuzco was said to receive fresh fish daily from the Pacific Ocean, carried by runners hundreds of miles over the mountains. After the fall of the Inca Empire, it took a couple of centuries, with the invention of the telegraph in the 1800s, for messages to move as fast again through Peru.

A journey along the Inca roadway would have been on foot. The Incas used no wheeled vehicles, and llamas served only as pack animals, not transportation. These surefooted relatives of the camel were ideally suited to the steep slopes of the Andes. Wherever possible, Inca roads ran straight, but in the Andes they zigzagged over mountain slopes. In places, retaining walls reinforced the roads' edges. Where slopes were especially steep, the road became a series of steps cut into the living rock.

BRIDGING THE GAP

Steep slopes were not the only challenge to builders of the Inca road system. Roads were halted by the many canyons, ravines, and rivers of the empire's mountainous terrain. Bridges filled such gaps in the system, continuing routes across such barriers.

TREKKING THE INCA TRAIL

The road the Incas traveled from their capital city, Cuzco, to Machu Picchu has become a popular destination for adventure tourism. Known as the Inca Trail, the route leads to an encounter with the past. Hikers along the thirty-three-mile trail find themselves up close and personal with Inca engineering works, including steep granite stairways and tunnels carved out of living rock.

The route also offers a challenge in endurance. The first pass on the trail is aptly named Abra de Huarmihuañusca in Spanish, or Warmiwanusq'a in the Quechua tongue. In either language, the meaning is "Dead Woman's Pass." This part of the trail crests at nearly fourteen thousand feet. At such heights, breathing becomes difficult. Also, temperatures plummet after nightfall, even in summer.

Hikers who brave the trail are rewarded with such views as glacier-covered peaks soaring above. Those seeking even more of a challenge can register for a twenty-seven and one-half-mile marathon along the route. *UltraRunning Magazine* touts this trek as "a unique blend of wilderness running and archaeological exploration."

To cross the deep river gorges in the Andes, suspension bridges were built. A suspension bridge hung high over the river below. This type of bridge was constructed using strong, thick ropes, or cables. To make cables, *mit'a* laborers twisted together vines and long stalks of grass, reinforced with twigs and sticks. They then braided the ropes to keep them from untwisting. Each cable measured about eight inches in diameter. Some cables became handrails. Others were lashed together to form a platform over which strips of wood or bamboo were fastened for a walkway. Workers used vines, cords, or strips of animal hide to secure

Inca bridges made of thick rope spanned deep river gorges, connecting the vast network of Inca roadways.

these strips to the underlying cables. Such relatively narrow bridges suited the foot traffic that was the norm during Inca times.

In his travelogue *Peru: Incidents of Travel and Exploration in the Land of the Incas*, published in 1877, George Squier remarked on the bridges built by the Incas:

Had the principle of the arch been well understood by the ancient inhabitants, who have left some of the finest stone-cutting and masonry to be found in the world, there is no doubt the interior of Peru would have abounded in bridges rivalling those of Rome in extent and beauty. As it was, occupying a country destitute of timber, they resorted to suspension bridges, no doubt precisely like those now constructed by their descendants and successors—bridges formed of cables of

This illustration shows how a suspension bridge spanned the Vilcumayu River north of Machu Picchu.

braided withes [slender branches], stretched from bank to bank. . . . Over these frail and swaying structures pass men and animals, the latter frequently with loads on their backs.[33]

Suspension bridges carried such caravans across the Urubamba River to Machu Picchu when the Incas inhabited it. A drawbridge then led directly to the sanctuary itself. Travelers approaching Machu Picchu from the Urubamba Valley encountered this bar to their entry. The trail here crossed the sheer face of a cliff. A rock wall was built out from the cliff, with a critically placed gap. Timbers, or logs, spanned the gap when visitors were welcome. However, the timbers could be removed to cut off the route from intruders.

This removable log crossing helped defend Machu Picchu against those who would violate its sacred ground. Similarly, the site's infrastructure helped protect its buildings against destructive natural forces. Its ruins would therefore endure, allowing future generations to marvel at the monumental architecture they displayed.

AN ARCHITECTURAL MARVEL

One of the Incas' greatest achievements was their architecture, in particular their stonework. Overall, the design of Inca buildings is plain and spare, but their stone walls dazzle the viewer with their jewel-like precision. Chronicler Bernabé Cobo commented that "the only remarkable part of these [Inca] buildings was the walls—but these were so amazing that it would be difficult for any who have not seen them to appreciate them."[34]

The spareness of the buildings at Machu Picchu allows them to blend beautifully with the environment. These buildings mirror the stark, primal power of the site's surrounding peaks. But such structures are not only tributes to nature. They are also monuments to the Incas and their empire.

A DEBT OWED

Like most human achievements, Inca architecture owed a debt to earlier civilizations. Precedents for the Incas' massive, expertly cut stone walls are found in the ruins of Tiahuanaco in present-day Bolivia. Tiahuanaco was the ceremonial center of an Andean civilization that thrived from around 700 B.C. to A.D. 1000. Huge, monumental buildings rise at the site. So enormous are the blocks of stone forming these buildings—some weighing up to a hundred tons—that a legend attributes Tiahuanaco's construction to a race of gods or giants at the beginning of time.

Probably encountering the ruins of Tiahuanaco on his march of conquest, Sapa Inca Pachacuti himself could not have failed to be awed by their magnificence. Evidently Pachacuti was inspired to reproduce Tiahuanaco's monumental scale in Inca settlements—starting with his capital city, Cuzco, which he

This undated painting shows the elegance and grandeur of the pre-Inca ruins of Tiahuanaco.

transformed from a smattering of rustic buildings into a great metropolis. Machu Picchu's majestic buildings also echo the grandeur of Tiahuanaco. Bernabé Cobo noted that "the Incas used [the temples of Tiahuanaco] as a model and design for the great structures of Cuzco and other parts of their empire."[35]

The conquest of the Lake Titicaca region, begun by Pachacuti and completed by his son Tupac Inca Yupanqui, supplied the Incas with more than just inspiration for monumental building projects like Machu Picchu. The Colla and Lupaca tribes then populating the region had inherited the stoneworking skills that built Tiahuanaco. Once absorbed into the Inca Empire, these tribes were subject to the Inca labor tax. Fulfilling their *mit'a* service in construction works, they applied their skill in shaping stone blocks and fitting them so tightly that even today a piece of paper cannot be wedged between them. Most scholars agree that descendants of Tiahuanaco helped achieve the superb masonry seen at Machu Picchu.

"Each Stone Outlined in a Frame of Sharp Shadow"

The skill of stoneworkers employed at Machu Picchu is evident in the tidy courses, or horizontal rows, of ashlars featured in many of its walls. Scholars suppose that this method evolved from the construction of walls using adobes, or bricks of sundried earth and straw. The Incas' conscious imitation of adobes in their coursed stone walls would explain the rounded surface of ashlars in these walls. When they dry, adobe bricks swell slightly. To reproduce this swelling, Inca masons sunk a stone's joints, or edges, by cutting them at a slant. This technique, known as rustication, angled the joints inward, so the stone appeared to bulge. "The effect of this rustication is magnificent," says author John Hemming, "with each stone outlined in a frame of sharp shadow in the clear Andean air."[36]

The relative size of ashlars produces another design feature of the Incas' coursed stone walls. Smaller stones appear in the courses toward the top, supported by larger ones in the rows below. Hiram Bingham described the effect this grading produced: "The lower courses, of particularly large ashlars, gave [the wall] a look of solidity. The upper courses, diminishing in size toward the top, lent grace and delicacy to the structure."[37]

One curious feature of coursed Inca walls, at Machu Picchu and elsewhere, is the occasional appearance of protuberances, or knobs, near the base of blocks. During the construction phase, these may have aided the positioning of levers to lower blocks in place or to raise them while preparing a base layer. Or perhaps the knobs served as ties for dragging blocks to the building site. If so, the question remains why they were not removed once they had done their job. Possibly they were hidden by the earthen ramps used to place stones, and then forgotten about. Still, it is not known why some were apparently removed and others left. According to John Hemming, they stayed for decorative purposes: "They provide sharp points of shadow to relieve the pattern of smooth surfaces and tight sunken joints of the best Inca stonework."[38]

As evidence that the Incas valued coursed walls, these carefully constructed walls dominate in buildings believed to be temples and palaces. In Machu Picchu, a building adjoining the Temple of the Sun offers an example. The walls of this building feature level layers of ashlars fitted with stunning precision. Because of its exquisite masonry, Bingham named the building the

CUT WITH AMAZING SKILL!

Sixteenth-century Spanish chronicler Bernabé Cobo expressed the amazement people still feel today at the Inca's ability to fit irregularly shaped boulders together with the precision of pieces in a jigsaw puzzle. In *Monuments of the Incas*, author John Hemming quotes Cobo:

> I can assure you that although they may appear rougher than walls of [coursed] ashlars, they seem to me to have been far more difficult to make. For, not being cut straight (apart from the outer face, which was as smooth as on the ashlars), and yet being so tightly joined to one another, one can well appreciate the amount of work involved in having them interlock in the way we see. Some are large and others small and both sorts are irregular in shape and structure, but they are still positioned with joints as delicate as those of coursed ashlars. Thus, if the top of one stone makes a curve or point there is a corresponding groove or cavity in the stone above to fit exactly into the other. Some stones have many angles and indentations all round their sides; but the stones they meet are cut in such a way that they interlock perfectly. Such a work must have been immensely laborious!

The Incas were skilled at fitting irregularly shaped boulders together, as evidenced in this doorway guarded by stone jaguars.

House of the Princess. More likely it housed the adjacent temple's head priest. In any case, one of its walls, made of blocks of white granite resembling marble, is particularly lovely. Bingham considered it "the most beautiful wall in all America."[39]

PIRCA

While coursed stone walls are a memorable feature of Machu Picchu, a different type of masonry known as *pirca* is also on view at the site. *Pirca* refers to fieldstones—locally gathered stones of various shapes and sizes—set in mortar. *Pirca* walls are seen in Machu Picchu's agricultural terraces as well as in modest dwellings clustered in the sanctuary's eastern sector. Craftspeople who supplied elite residents with luxury goods probably lived in these dwellings. As a building technique, *pirca* was well suited to the stony, relatively treeless Andes.

Pirca *walls follow the natural contour of Machu Picchu's eastern hillsides.*

    Pirca walls required less effort to build than walls consisting of stone courses. After chipping the fieldstones to fit together crudely, workers held them in place with mortar rather than making sure to interlock them tightly. The mortar consisted of clay and earth mixed with very small rocks. Reports that the Incas sometimes used melted silver or gold as mortar led the Spanish conquistadors to tear down many walls in Inca structures. Whatever it was made of, the mortar was applied in a layer, which workers then overlaid with fieldstones. In addition, mortar was placed in the center of the wall, joining the inner surfaces of the wall faces. Mortar also served as fill for the interior of the wall.

The magnificent stonework featured in coursed walls needed no further finishing. However, *pirca* walls with their rougher surface may have been covered with a stuccolike mud or clay surface to present a more smooth and uniform surface. This allowed the walls to be painted, either red, white, or yellow ocher—bright colors favored by the Incas.

Machu Picchu's royal tomb is adorned with finely carved stones fitted between natural granite boulders.

JIGSAW-PUZZLE WALLS

Machu Picchu offers examples of still another style of Inca stonework. This style, known as polygonal, features irregularly shaped stones whose edges have been worked to fit together like pieces in a jigsaw puzzle. Besides an unusual look, polygonal masonry provides a lot of strength to structures. The Incas often used this type of masonry to build containing walls for platforms and terraces. Generally, very large stones were involved.

A marvelous example of polygonal masonry at Machu Picchu appears in a building that Bingham identified as a royal tomb. Here the mummies of the Inca royal family may have rested. In one wall of this building, workers fitted stones in an hourglass shape between the living granite rock.

The virtuosity of Inca stoneworkers is also on display in what Bingham called the Ornamental Chamber. This space is enclosed by an extension of a wall belonging to Machu Picchu's principal temple, believed to have honored Viracocha, the creator god of Andean myth. In one corner lies a block with thirty-two angles, or facets, carved into its surface, in three dimensions. "This isn't building," declares author Richard Danbury, "it's sculpture." [40]

DECEPTIVELY LOW WALLS

In addition to stone, Inca builders used adobe, that is, earth and straw shaped into bricks and sun dried. However, in the rainy Andean highlands, adobe is less well preserved, so adobe is less prevalent than stone at Machu Picchu. Lacking the solidity of stone, adobe is more susceptible to water erosion.

In Inca times, adobe presumably formed the upper part of walls at Machu Picchu, supported by rain-resistant stone foundations. Buildings at the site therefore once stood higher than their ruins now suggest. Lacking any trace of adobe, "the walls seem low to us," note Graziano Gasparini and Luise Margolies, authors of *Inca Architecture*, "and the interior space of the surviving chambers is deceptive." [41] The adobe probably eroded away once the roof protecting it collapsed.

THATCH ROOFS

Also missing in Machu Picchu's buildings today are their thatch roofs—except where such roofs have been restored to offer

MAIZE

Maize, a kind of corn, was a staple of the Inca diet. It formed the basis for various dishes, including a stew that chronicler Bernabé Cobo called *motepatasca*. *Motepatasca* was prepared by cooking maize with herbs and chili peppers until the kernels burst open. The Incas also ate a kind of corn bread baked in ashes or else boiled. Popcorn was prized as a delicacy.

Because of its mythic origin, maize also played an important role in Inca ritual. According to Inca mythology, maize was the gift of Mama Huaca, sister and wife of the first Inca, Manco Capac. Mama Huaca is believed to have brought ears of corn with her when she emerged with her brothers and sisters from the cave of Tambo-Toqo, the mythic birthplace of the Inca tribe—kernels of maize were in fact called "cave seeds." *Chicha*, a mildly intoxicating drink made from maize, was regularly served at Inca ceremonies. The Hatun Raimi, a festival lasting up to twenty days that marked the annual maize and potato harvest, featured *taquis*, or drinking feasts, in which large amounts of *chicha* were consumed.

Women consecrated to holy service prepared the ceremonial *chicha* by first chewing the maize kernels and then spitting the pulp into a jar of warm water. Enzymes in the women's saliva started the fermenting process by breaking down sugars in the maize. Fermenting was allowed to continue for several days.

Mama Huaca (pictured) was believed to have brought the first ears of corn to the Inca people.

tourists a clearer picture of authentic Inca architecture, such as atop a building identified as a guardhouse, which overlooks the site from high up on Machu Picchu mountain. A grassy material, thatch is far from permanent. Still, according to chronicler Pedro de Cieza de León, the Incas wove their thatch so densely, it could survive many years unless destroyed by fire. Indeed, the thatch covering royal buildings was as thick as six feet. Inca thatch could also be very elaborate. One building in the Yucay Valley, north of Cuzco, featured a conical, or beehive-shaped, thatch roof soaring to more than sixty feet.

To keep their thatch roofs from blowing away without the use of nails, the Incas tied them with fiber or willow ropes to stone pegs projecting from a building's outer walls. The part of the peg flush with the wall was shaped roughly square for a firm hold, while the outer end was rounded so as not to cut into the rope. These pegs were placed at right angles to the slope of the gable, or triangular top of the wall.

GABLES

Gables are commonly seen in buildings at Machu Picchu. Gabled buildings required a complex roof frame. Central to this frame, a ridgepole, or main roof beam, rested both its ends on the tops of the gables, which formed the two shorter sides of the building. Supporting this pole, as well as the weight of the thatch, was a series of crossbeams. Chronicler Garcilaso de la Vega described the process the Incas followed in laying a gabled roof structure:

> They set loose on the walls all the timbers that served as framing: for the top of [the frame] in place of [using] nails, they tied it with strong ropes. . . . On these first timbers they place[d] those that served as purlins and rafters [crossbeams], also tied one to another and that to another; over all they laid the covering of grass. . . . The roof itself served as a cornice for the wall, so that it would not get wet. . . . [T]hey clipped all the grass that extended beyond the walls very evenly.[42]

The steep pitches to the Incas' gabled roofs also helped protect the walls of buildings from the eroding effects of rainwater. In addition, such high, pointy roofs reduced the thrust on walls. The sharper the angle at the ridge, or top, the less the pressure on the walls below.

A MISSING WALL

Given the rainfall common to the Andes, it may be surprising to find buildings open on one side at Machu Picchu, but, in fact, many three-walled buildings appear at the site. In such

The ruins of this three-walled masma *are missing a wooden beam and a thatched roof, which would typically have run the length of the building.*

buildings, known as *masmas*, the roof slope of the open side rests on a wood beam. Each end of the beam is set into the base of the triangle forming the gable at each side wall. In larger buildings of this type, called *kallankas*, a monolithic stone pillar or series of pillars, placed near the middle of the beam, helped support the roof. Garcilaso de la Vega estimated that *kallankas*, on average, were "some two hundred paces long and fifty to sixty feet wide,"[43] and according to chronicler Cristóbal de Molina, "a great quantity of people could be housed in each of these [*kallankas*], which were very well covered, clean and [well fitted]."[44]

Masmas were probably occupied only part of the time. Filled with light during the daytime, some may have served as workspaces. At Machu Picchu, a *masma* dominates the center of the compound that Bingham named the Mortar Group. Another of the city's *masmas* is considered a guardhouse, because, at its vantage point high above the site, it stood at the junction of paths to Machu Picchu during Inca times.

Kallankas, wrote chronicler Garcilaso de la Vega, "served as places of assembly for festivals and dances when the weather was too rainy to permit [the Incas] to hold these in the open air."[45] In Machu Picchu overlooking the main plaza, where public ceremonies usually were staged, is a *kallanka* believed to be Machu Picchu's principal temple, honoring Viracocha, the creator god of the Incas. It occupies the north end of a plaza on a ridge to the west of the main plaza. At the eastern end of this smaller plaza lies another *kallanka*, its open end, like that of the principal temple, looking out over the main plaza below. This *kallanka* is known as the Temple of the Three Windows.

Other than its obvious significance to the Incas who built it, mystery continues to surround the Temple of the Three Windows. For one thing, the windows are unusually large, "far too large for comfort in this cold climate,"[46] concluded Bingham.

This kallanka *features Machu Picchu's principal temple (top left).*

Trapezoidal windows like this one are a distinct feature of Inca masonry.

Compounding the mystery, the three windows were originally five. Inca architects ordered two of the windows filled up, but why they did so is a question still unanswered.

AN INCA HALLMARK

Like all windows found in the ruins of Machu Picchu, those in the Temple of the Three Windows are trapezoidal in shape, though with rounded lower corners and subtly curved sides to widen the view. Trapezoidal openings—including doorways and niches, or recesses in walls—are a distinctively Inca feature. "It was so common and so peculiarly Inca that it became their hallmark," writes John Hemming, "the sure sign that a structure was built during the Inca era."[47]

In a trapezoidal opening, the sill, or bottom, is longer than the lintel, or top, and the jambs, or sides, slope in as they rise. This shape is structurally advantageous. The weight supported by the lintel is lessened, and the thrust is spread to either side of the opening. A sturdier structure is the result.

Trapezoidal openings served an aesthetic as well as practical purpose. "Niches must have had a strong appeal to the disciplined minds of the Incas," Hemming writes. "They were functional, useful and decorative—breaking the monotony of a bare wall with the symmetry of a row of classical columns."[48]

When positioned at chest height on a building's inside walls, niches were useful for storage. Inca buildings had little in the way of furniture, so niches took the place of closets, bureaus, shelves, cupboards, and tables. Because they served as multipurpose containers, the sizes of niches varied widely. The unusually large niches in what Bingham considered Machu Picchu's royal tomb might have displayed mummies, bundled in Inca fashion with knees to chin. Smaller niches on the side walls of Machu Picchu's fountains probably held jugs used to pour water for ceremonial purposes.

A Rectangular Plan

Another typical shape in Inca construction is the rectangle. Inca buildings almost always follow a rectangular plan. Archaeologists suspect that Sapa Inca Pachacuti pirated from a neighboring people known as the Huari the layout of the *kancha*, a group of buildings arranged within a rectangular enclosure, to streamline his grand-scale building projects.

The *kancha* formed the basic building unit of Inca settlements, including Machu Picchu. These all-purpose units may have served variously as temple grounds, living quarters, or production sites devoted to such crafts as weaving. As living quarters, a *kancha* may have housed an extended family.

Generally surrounding a type of courtyard, buildings in a *kancha* numbered up to eight or more. Machu Picchu's commoners, concentrated in the urban sector's eastern end, probably gathered in their courtyards most of the day. As long as the sun was out, few would have wanted to spend time inside their small, dark, thatched dwellings. Little light entered these humble buildings, which typically lacked windows. They also lacked chimneys or other outlets for smoke. Chances are that cooking was done outdoors, on clay stoves. For fuel, these stoves burned wood and sticks when available—which was probably hardly at all, because in the Andes trees are rare. Therefore, llama dung was mostly used for fuel. In fact, the *kancha*'s enclosure provided a convenient corral for llamas.

Only the most important structures at Machu Picchu employed solid doorframes.

ENTRANCES AND EXITS

Besides chimneys, Inca buildings lacked rooms leading from one to the other. Garcilaso de la Vega reports that the Incas "did not connect rooms together, but made them all separate each one by itself. . . . [T]he four walls of stone or adobe, of any house or buildings, large or small, were made completely finished inside because they did not know how to connect one room with another."[49] One-room buildings predominated in Inca settlements, including Machu Picchu. Doorways were usually found in one of the long sides of the rectangle.

Doorways to most Inca buildings used no locks. A stick across the opening announced the residents were away, so visitors should return at a later time. People did not concern themselves about security not only because under Inca rule they were guaranteed such necessities as food and clothing, but also because most had few possessions of their own worth stealing. Personal belongings were limited to dishes, cooking pots, clothing, and shawl pins. Still, the absence of locks in Inca buildings astonished the Spaniards who conquered the Inca Empire; one conquistador noted in his will, in a section addressed to Spain's King Philip: "When [the Incas] saw that we placed locks and keys in our doors they understood that it was from fear of thieves and when they saw that we had thieves amongst us they despised us."[50]

Although they lacked locks, important Inca structures were supplied with solid doorways. In the building identified as Machu Picchu's Temple of the Sun, for example, a door frame apparently hung from a stone ring fixed above the lintel. The door itself consisted of interlaced poles, or else an animal's hide. To help secure the door, a crossbeam would have been lashed to stone pegs sunk into the doorjambs. To fasten the crossbeam more securely, Inca masons sometimes anchored the pegs within hollows carved into the sides of the doorway. Workers first primed the rock to be hollowed out with water and sand, in an effort to help dissolve it. They then bore into the rock by repeatedly revolving pieces of bamboo between their palms.

EXCEPTIONS TO THE RULE

Despite the Incas' preference for rectangular structures, exceptions existed. Machu Picchu's Temple of the Sun, for example, has a semicircular wall. The walls of another building at the site combine with a natural rock outcrop to resemble outstretched wings. The rock itself is carved to look like the head, beak, and ruff, or feather collar, of a condor, South America's largest bird.

The building incorporating this condor-shaped rock spreads over a series of underground caves. These caves may have served as prison vaults. Chronicler Felipé Guamán Poma de Ayala described an Inca prison as "constructed below ground in the form of a crypt, very dark, where they raised snakes, poisonous serpents, pumas, jaguars, bears, foxes, dogs, wildcats, vultures, eagles. . . —creatures that could be used to punish criminals and delinquents. . . . Those who committed serious crimes were placed in those vaults in order that the beasts would devour them alive." Poma de Ayala added that suspected criminals were punished by "tying the hands and feet with a cord and twisting it to obtain confession."[51] Walls of the building do show niches large enough to hold a human being. In addition, the niches' stone frames feature holes allowing for the tying of cords mentioned by Poma de Ayala. Or the niches may have served as sites where habitual wrongdoers were executed, according to Bernabé Cobo, "by hanging with their heads downward and being left hanging this way till they died."[52]

Alternatively, religious ceremonies rather than harsh punishments may have been carried out in this building. The condor stone was possibly an altar, though it lacks the customary grooves for draining away sacrificial fluids. If the building were indeed a temple, the underground caverns probably served as a tomb. In that case, the niches held mummies, not criminals.

QOLLQAS

Another exception to the standard rectangular building form was the *qollqa.* This storehouse or granary sometimes had a rounded shape, like a silo. Chronicler Bernabé Cobo reported that *qollqas* were "set in a line like little towers, very neatly and

"NONE SUFFERED WANT"

Their system of storehouses shows that the Incas were as skilled administrators as they were builders. Some storehouses, or *qollqas*, supported members of the Sapa Inca's household. Others supplied the Inca army. Still others stockpiled food for distribution in times of famine. Spanish chronicler Bernabé Cobo, quoted in John Hemming's book *Monuments of the Incas*, described how the system of storehouses functioned in Inca society:

> [The *qollqas*] provided food for the [Sapa] Inca and his relatives and attendant lords. They also supplied the garrisons, patrols and fighting men, who received no pay apart from food and clothing—each soldier was paid with two sets of clothing each year. The [Sapa] Inca would also grant chiefs permission to distribute part of the cloth and food in the stores in their districts to keep their subjects contented. . . . Once a province had enough for its own needs [the Incas] provided for the requirements of other districts. Supplies were thus taken from one province to another—they often transported stores from the plains to the mountains and in the opposite direction. They took great care over this. It was done so systematically and efficiently that there was no lack in any area and none suffered want, even in lean years. . . . Whatever was left over or not needed was kept in storehouses for a time of need. There was always quite enough when such times occurred: for they sometimes stored food for ten or twelve years.

symmetrically and spaced two or three yards apart from one another."[53] Apparently this spacing prevented a fire sparked in one structure from spreading to the others in the line.

Given the *qollqas'* purely practical purpose, functionality was the key to their design. Rough fieldstone, rather than evenly coursed ashlars, formed their walls. A ventilation system was designed to preserve the storehouses' contents against spoilage. Ducts, or channels, under the floor and near the roof allowed constant air circulation through the structure. Having devised a way to dehydrate food for storage, the Incas stockpiled frozen or cooked dried potatoes, as well as jerked, or sun-dried, strips of llama meat. Foods able to be eaten without prior cooking—including maize, sweet potatoes, and chili peppers—could also be stored.

Machu Picchu's agricultural sector features buildings that have been identified as *qollqas*. It has been calculated that Machu Picchu's agricultural terraces would have failed to produce enough food for residents when their numbers reached the site's maximum capacity—estimated to be twelve hundred. Access to the contents of *qollqas* would have proved critical, then, to the city's survival.

THE STATE AS ARCHITECT

Ensuring their uniform character, Inca settlements including Machu Picchu were constructed under the supervision of government architects. The nineteenth-century archaeologist Alexander von Humboldt remarked, "It is impossible to examine carefully a single edifice of the Incas attentively without recognizing the same type in all the rest that exist in the length of the Andes. . . . It seems as if a single architect built this great number of monuments."[54] In reply, Graziano Gasparini and Luise Margolies write: "In fact, a single architect did build that great number of monuments. A single architect—the state— selected and imposed the limited repertoire of technical and formal solutions."[55] Rarely was effort wasted on purely decorative flourishes. Inca buildings are conspicuously bare of moldings or carvings or fanciful representations of plants, animals, or human beings.

The uniform nature of Inca architecture, clearly on display at Machu Picchu, apparently served the Incas' imperial ambitions. As a practical matter, standardized architectural forms such as the *kancha* could easily be reproduced throughout the expanding Inca Empire. Symbolically, a standard, official style signaled Inca rule over widespread areas.

Contributing to the uniformity of what has become known as classic Inca architecture, its development was restricted to the eighty years or so of the flowering of the empire. The Spanish conquest in the sixteenth century put a swift end to its evolution.

SURVIVAL OF
THE SITE

The beauty and allure of Machu Picchu have made it one of the world's most famous ruins. But fame has been both a blessing and a curse for Machu Picchu. Business interests are as enthusiastic about exploiting its mystique as scholars and spiritual seekers are to probe its mysteries.

As guardians of the site, the people of Peru must balance its commercial use with its preservation as a symbol of their heritage. This dilemma is compounded by the poverty faced by most Peruvians, making the infusion of cash a powerful incentive to sell Machu Picchu as a marketing tool—for tourism as well as corporate advertising.

"A MARKETING MECCA"

Marketing and advertising firms have been eager to connect Machu Picchu's exotic, mystical appeal with clients' products in the public mind. "The spectacular ruins of Machu Picchu," notes MSNBC News Services, "has become a marketing mecca."[56] Such marketability comes at a cost to the site, however. In September 2000 a thousand-pound crane being used to film a beer commercial at Machu Picchu toppled over and chipped off an edge of the Intihuatana. Although the piece broken off measured a mere 2.8 inches, repair required advanced restoration techniques. Moreover, the Intihuatana is not just any stone. It is—or was—the only intact Hitching Post of the Sun remaining after the Spanish conquest; crusading Spaniards lopped off the tops of any Intihuatanas they could find as an insult to the Inca worship they represented. "Machu Picchu is the heart of our archaeological heritage and the Intihuatana is the heart of Machu

Tourists take in the beauty and majesty of Machu Picchu.

Picchu. [The makers of the commercial have] struck at our sacred inheritance,"[57] remarked Peruvian archaeologist Federico
Kaufmann Doig.

Peru's Instituto Nacional de Cultura (National Institute of
Culture), or INC, blamed the film production crew completely
for the incident. According to Gustavo Manrique, Cuzco's INC
director, the permit issued to the crew specified that only light
equipment was allowed on the site. Manrique accused the crew
of sneaking the heavy crane into Machu Picchu at dawn to
avoid being caught violating the terms of the permit.

The shoot, peddling the Peruvian beer company Cervesur,
was not the first to use Machu Picchu as the backdrop of a sales
pitch. The U.S. publicity firm J. Walter Thompson, which shot
the Cervesur ad, had filmed commercials there before. Models
have posed for fashion shoots among the ruins, too.

A NATIONAL HISTORICAL SANCTUARY

Commercial use of Machu Picchu continues despite its official
recognition as a site of historical value. In 1981 the government

of Peru established Machu Picchu as a National Historical Sanctuary. The government took this action to protect not only the ruins but also their natural surroundings. The architecture of Machu Picchu is fully integrated with the environment, and any threat to the environment threatens the integrity of the site as a whole. In addition, Machu Picchu is home to plant and animal life that have been found nowhere else in the world, including species of orchids, insects, and butterflies. In bamboo thickets in

THE NEW 7 WONDERS OF THE WORLD PROJECT

Machu Picchu was recently in the running to be named one of the New Seven Wonders of the World. The original Seven Wonders were marvels of building and construction produced by ancient civilizations, and only one of them—the pyramids of Giza in Egypt—can still be seen today. Among the twenty-five contestants, besides Machu Picchu, vying to be counted among the world's top seven architectural feats since the compiling in the new list: the Great Wall of China, the Leaning Tower of Pisa, India's Taj Mahal, France's Eiffel Tower, Cambodia's Angkor Wat, Mexico's Chichén Itzá, the Golden Gate Bridge in San Francisco Bay, and the Statue of Liberty in New York Harbor.

The New 7 Wonders of the World Project was launched in the year 2000. According to the project's website (www.newsevenwonders.com), the dawn of the third millennium marked "an appropriate time to determine the new seven symbols of the most important human accomplishments of the last 2000 years."

Only one man—Philon of Byzantium—chose the original Seven Wonders; the selection of the New Seven Wonders, however, was put to a vote over the Internet. By mid-2002, about 6 million votes from more than two hundred nations had been logged on the New 7 Wonders of the World Project website. According to the project's developers, headed by Swiss-born explorer and filmmaker Bernard Weber: "The great success expressed in the number of votes received . . . has strengthened our belief that we are on the verge of bringing about a meaningful dialogue between the citizens of the world."

the area, a new species of bird has been discovered: a wren with the scientific name *Thryothorus.* Machu Picchu also harbors the spectacled bear, a threatened species of wildlife.

Management of the sanctuary's 80,500 acres faces a number of challenges. For one, administration of the preserve is divided among seven ministries of the government, making it difficult to coordinate policies and practices. Also, about two-thirds of the sanctuary is being farmed, thus increasing the danger of accidental fires. Local farmers have had to be discouraged from setting fire to the neighboring forest in order to turn it into farmland.

FIRE PREVENTION

The hazard of fire to Machu Picchu cannot be ignored. In early August 1997, a forest fire engulfed Huayna Picchu, charring

A Peruvian man struggles to clean stones bordering Machu Picchu after they were charred by a fire in August 1997.

trail ways, terraces, and walls built on its heights. In addition, the fire damaged the Inca drawbridge leading to the monument. The fire, sparked at a nearby hydroelectric plant on the Urubamba River, raged for an entire week before being brought under control. Fortunately, firefighters snuffed out the blaze before it reached the saddle ridge of Machu Picchu. Still, flames scorched several hundred acres bordering the site.

Efforts have since been launched to avoid another major fire. The director of the Cuzco office of Peru's Instituto Nacional de Cultura proposed a network of water-storage reservoirs and piping to supply extra water to the site for dousing flames. He also reviewed plans for satellites to monitor Machu Picchu and its surroundings for signs of fire. In the meantime, workers cleaned the stone structures blackened by smoke, and the site again opened to the tourist trade.

A VERY PRESSING PROBLEM

Among the most pressing problems facing the managers of the National Historical Sanctuary of Machu Picchu is how to handle the tourist trade. Costly restrictions on tourism must be weighed against pressures from preservationists to maintain the integrity of the site. Tourism remains a major source of income for Peru's poverty-stricken population.

Yet without some limitations on tourist traffic, what centuries of choking plant life failed to accomplish might just be achieved by crowds of human beings within decades: that is, serious damage to the site. Up to 3,000 visitors a day flock to Machu Picchu, while scholars estimate that in Inca times it housed at most 1,200, and that only seasonally—most of the year its residents numbered between 600 and 700. The question has been raised whether the site can continue to support a daily crush of people. Conservationists have already pointed out the danger of polluting air particles eating away the rock forming Machu Picchu's priceless structures. Such pollutants arrive with the buses that deposit tourists at the site. Currently tourists not hiking the Inca Trail to Machu Picchu arrive after a twenty-five-minute bus ride up a winding dirt road, bare of railings, dubbed "Zig-Zag Bingham Road." Another source of pollution is garbage left by visitors to the ruins. Adding to conservationists' concerns, the owners of the Machu Picchu Sanctuary Lodge, just outside the entrance gate, are planning to enlarge the facility and thus

SPECTACLED BEAR

Among the wildlife protected within the National Historical Sanctuary of Machu Picchu is the only bear native to South America, the spectacled bear. The animal—also known as the Andean bear—is endangered, mostly because of the loss of its habitat, or home environment, to human settlement. The spectacled bear gets its name from the distinctive white or yellow markings around its eyes and snout—resembling eyeglasses, or spectacles. The shape and extent of the markings vary from one bear to another: On some animals, the markings extend to the neck and chest, while on others they hardly appear at all, so the face looks almost entirely black.

While the spectacled bear is in danger of extinction today, in Inca times it was revered. Because it lives in the high altitudes of the Andes, it was seen by Andean peoples, including the Incas, as a mediator, or link, between the spirits of the lower regions (humans) and the upper regions (the gods); the people of the Andes even believed the bear helped preserve order and stability in times of turmoil, to the benefit of humankind. The winter solstice, when the sun lies at its greatest distance from the earth, was considered to be such a dark, perilous time. Still today, during the winter solstice (June in Peru), some Andean natives dress like bears to participate in a redemptive ritual.

Chances are, visitors to Machu Picchu will not see a spectacled bear. They tend to be shy as well as solitary. Superb climbers, they spend much of their time in trees. There they feast on fruit, their main food source.

increase the problem of waste disposal at the site—despite protests from UNESCO, which has declared the ruins a World Heritage Site.

Concerns have also been raised about safeguarding the Inca Trail. Preservationists have charged, for example, that the weight of millions of pairs of hiking boots is threatening the longevity of the trail. The trail, after all, was designed for bare or sandaled feet.

THE CABLE CAR CONTROVERSY

Despite the fact that tourism levels are pushing capacity, in 1999 the government agreed to a plan that would increase the number of visitors to Machu Picchu by 20 percent a year. The plan involved running a pair of cable cars from the Urubamba Valley floor fifteen hundred feet up to Machu Picchu. At the rate of six minutes a ride, carrying about forty-five passengers each, the two cars promised to ferry up to four hundred tourists an hour to and from the site.

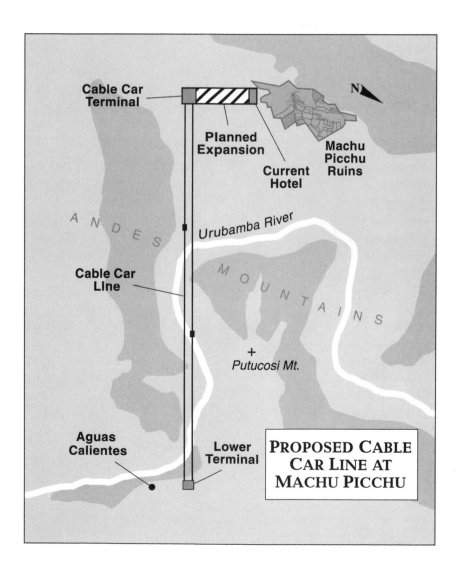

PROPOSED CABLE
CAR LINE AT
MACHU PICCHU

The project's developers, Orient Express, insisted that their plan would ultimately preserve the ruins. They argued that the cable car system would help regulate the flow of visitors to the site and so prevent crowds from pressing in on it all at once. In addition, the cable cars would replace the buses that have been blamed for polluting the air around Machu Picchu.

News of the cable car project and its proposed boost to tourism stirred controversy. Environmentalists charged that building a cable car terminal could raise the risk of landslides in the area. Others expressed outrage over modern structures marring the ancient Inca monument. "Machu Picchu is not just another tourist site," says Peter Frost, a Cuzco-based tourist guide. "You can't separate it from its surroundings. When you break that sacred geography, you break the harmony of the experience."[58]

A report by UNESCO, issued in February 2000, echoed Frost's concerns. It states: "The cable car system . . . would very seriously affect the World Heritage values, authenticity and integrity of the . . . citadel and its surrounding landscape" it goes on to recommend that "no new construction of infrastructure be introduced in the area."[59] To sound the alarm even louder, that year UNESCO placed Machu Picchu on its list of the 100 Most Endangered Heritage Sites.

In response to the growing controversy, the Peruvian government put the cable car plan on hold in the spring of 2001. UNESCO responded in July by removing Machu Picchu from their Most Endangered list.

UNESCO may have acted too soon. By August, Peru's vice minister for tourism, Ramiro Salas, was proposing an alternative cable car system, one whose approach to the ruins would be opposite to that of the original plan. How this would be an improvement from the previous route was not made clear.

In fact, opponents promptly voiced their concerns that the route would be even more disastrous than the one proposed before. First, they claimed, the system's lower terminal would be built in an area particularly prone to landslides. In addition, the upper terminal would be placed in the ruins themselves. Finally, tourists using the cable cars would bypass the village of Aguas Calientes, seriously damaging the local economy. The route through the village is currently the only land route, other than the Inca Trail, to Machu Picchu. Hotels, restaurants, and sou-

AGUAS CALIENTES

Built in the shadow of Machu Picchu, Aguas Calientes is a way station, or stopover, for visitors to the celebrated site. Running through the center of town are railroad tracks. Daily, a train travels these tracks linking Aguas Calientes to the ancient Inca capital of Cuzco. Tourists board the train in Cuzco for a four-hour ride to Aguas Calientes, where they continue on to the ruins in a tour bus for another twenty-five minutes. The only other land route to Machu Picchu is by way of the rigorous Inca Trail.

Aguas Calientes's railroad tracks serve double duty as the town's main, and in fact only, street. Once the train has chugged away from the platform, people stride onto the tracks. The tracks lead travelers bound for Machu Picchu to the edge of town, where they can catch one of the four buses that climbs the road to the site. Lining the train tracks are hotels that host overnight visitors to the ruins. Also strewn along the railway are makeshift storefronts, from pizza parlors to travel agencies and souvenir shops. According to Max Milligan, in his book *Realm of the Incas*, Aguas Calientes was built "in a great hurry with no particular plan apart from tourist dollars." Souvenirs sold at Aguas Calientes include silk-screened T-shirts and stone-carved pumas, or mountain lions, which the Incas revered.

Paralleling one of the railroad platforms is the Urubamba River. Local women still wash clothes in its waters. Ramshackle homes made of wood, brick, mud, and sticks cluster along a footpath following the course of the river.

venir shops in Aguas Calientes are almost entirely supported by visitors to the ruins.

A SHARED GOAL

Proponents of tourism and preservation share a goal of offering visitors to Machu Picchu an authentic experience of Inca culture. In the interests of tourism as well as historic preservation, the Peruvian government has restored several structures on the site. The thatch roofing on the guardhouse on Machu Picchu mountain, for example, has been reconstructed, so it now offers

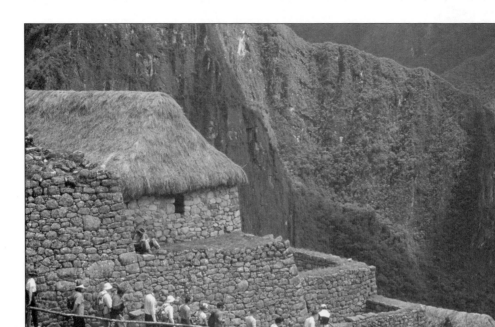

Archaeologists and government officials agree that visitors should continue to enjoy Machu Picchu, but tourism at the site must be regulated.

visitors shelter on rainy days. Other buildings with reconstructed roofs include a *qollqa* in the agricultural section and one of the buildings flanking the Sacred Rock. Besides appealing to tourists' desire to experience the site in its original state, a restored roof helps preserve a building's walls from the weakening effects of rainwater.

Alarmed at the possible loss of a monument to Peru's heritage—which is also a huge tourist draw—the Peruvian government is finally considering regulations on travel to the site. Proposals include fee increases to enter the Inca Trail. In addition, individual hikers may be forced to register with guided groups to more easily control traffic along the route.

At Machu Picchu itself, officials are planning to restrict visitors to a fixed circuit of tours. The aim is to prevent people from wandering unsupervised through the ruins. Already, camping is forbidden on the site.

A SYMBOL OF LOST STORIES

Crowds of tourists overrunning Machu Picchu threaten the sanctuary beyond the physical damage they may cause. Something more elusive but not any less significant may be at stake. Without any check on tourism, Machu Picchu risks turning into what author Richard Bangs calls "McPicchu." Disgusted by the "hoards" of tourists swarming the ruins on his visit to the site, Bangs writes, "I hated being herded around a theme park."[60]

But, ultimately, Machu Picchu may have a way of surviving efforts to package it for mass consumption. Bangs's climb up precipitous Huayna Picchu rewarded him with a view of the site encompassing not only the "antlike tourists scurrying among the ruins," but also the rapids of the Urubamba swirling below and the glacier-capped peak of Salcantay in the distance—causing him to conclude: "The only thing I could see clearly was that Machu Picchu cannot be decoded, that it stands in as a [symbolic] shorthand for the whole universe of lost stories."[61] Its many mysteries are part of the enduring appeal of Machu Picchu, echoing in the expanses of its mountain home.

NOTES

Introduction: Mute Witness to a Lost World

1. Elías J. Mujica, "Machu Picchu." *World Heritage Review* 11. www.unesco.org.

Chapter 1: Reclaimed from the Jungle

2. Quoted in John Hemming, *Monuments of the Incas.* Boston: Little, Brown, 1982, p. 131.
3. Hemming, *Monuments of the Incas*, p. 119.
4. Hiram Bingham, *Lost City of the Incas: The Story of Machu Picchu and Its Builders.* New York: Duell, Sloan and Pearce, 1948, p. 161.
5. Bingham, *Lost City of the Incas*, p. 161.
6. Bingham, *Lost City of the Incas*, p. 161.
7. Hiram Bingham, *In the Wonderland of Peru: The Work Accomplished by the Peruvian Expedition of 1912, Under the Auspices of Yale University and the National Geographic Society.* Washington, DC: National Geographic Society, 1913, p. 408.
8. Bingham, *Lost City of the Incas*, p. 165.
9. Bingham, *In the Wonderland of Peru*, p. 408.
10. Bingham, *Lost City of the Incas*, p. 166.
11. Bingham, *In the Wonderland of Peru*, p. 451.
12. Quoted in Bingham, *In the Wonderland of Peru*, pp. 431, 438.
13. Bingham, *Lost City of the Incas*, p. 203.

Chapter 2: A Puzzling Purpose

14. Bingham, *Lost City of the Incas*, p. 251.
15. Bingham, *Lost City of the Incas*, p. 251.
16. Quoted in Hemming, *Monuments of the Incas*, p. 44.
17. Quoted in Hemming, *Monuments of the Incas*, p. 133.
18. Max Milligan, *Realm of the Incas.* New York: Universe Publishing, 2001, p. 157.
19. Quoted in John Hyslop, *Inka Settlement Planning.* Austin: University of Texas Press, 1990, p. 110.
20. Bingham, *Lost City of the Incas*, p. 35.

21. Quoted in Hemming, *Monuments of the Incas*, p. 149.

22. Val Jon Farris, *Inca Fire! Light of the Masters: A True and Inspiring Spiritual Adventure*. Auburn, CA: Keystone Group, 1999, pp. 45, 47.

23. Farris, *Inca Fire!*, p. 47.

Chapter 3: Laying the Groundwork

24. Quoted in Hyslop, *Inka Settlement Planning*, p. 27.

25. Hyslop, *Inka Settlement Planning*, p. 28.

26. Quoted in Graziano Gasparini and Luise Margolies, *Inca Architecture*, trans. Patricia J. Lyon. Bloomington: Indiana University Press, 1980, p. 306.

27. Quoted in Gasparini and Margolies, *Inca Architecture*, p. 305.

28. Quoted in Hemming, *Monuments of the Incas*, p. 23.

29. Bingham, *Lost City of the Incas*, p. 179.

30. Kenneth R. Wright and Alfredo Valencia Zegarra, *Machu Picchu: A Civil Engineering Marvel*. Reston, VA: American Society of Civil Engineers Press, 2000, p. 38.

31. Quoted in Hemming, *Monuments of the Incas*, pp. 23, 26.

32. Quoted in John Hemming, *Machu Picchu*. New York: Newsweek, 1981, p. 92.

33. Quoted in Carmen Bernand, *The Incas: People of the Sun*. New York: Harry N. Abrams, 1994, p. 173.

Chapter 4: An Architectural Marvel

34. Quoted in Hemming, *Monuments of the Incas*, p. 13.

35. Quoted in Hemming, *Monuments of the Incas*, p. 26.

36. Hemming, *Monuments of the Incas*, p. 26.

37. Bingham, *Lost City of the Incas*, p. 165.

38. Hemming, *Monuments of the Incas*, p. 33.

39. Quoted in Richard Danbury, *The Inca Trail: Cuzco and Machu Picchu*. Hinhead, Surrey, UK: Trailblazer Publications, 2000, p. 227.

40. Danbury, *The Inca Trail*, p. 222.

41. Gasparini and Margolies, *Inca Architecture*, p. 309.

42. Quoted in Gasparini and Margolies, *Inca Architecture*, pp. 312–13.

43. Quoted in Hemming, *Monuments of the Incas*, p. 36.

44. Quoted in Hemming, *Monuments of the Incas*, p. 36.

45. Quoted in Hemming, *Monuments of the Incas*, p. 36.

46. Bingham, *In the Wonderland of Peru*, p. 512.

47. Hemming, *Monuments of the Incas*, p. 28.

48. Hemming, *Monuments of the Incas*, p. 33.

49. Quoted in Gasparini and Margolies, *Inca Architecture*, p. 134.

50. Quoted in Bingham, *Lost City of the Incas*, p. 8.

51. Quoted in Hemming, *Monuments of the Incas*, p. 155.

52. Quoted in Hemming, *Monuments of the Incas*, p. 155.

53. Quoted in Hemming, *Monuments of the Incas*, p. 46.

54. Quoted in Gasparini and Margolies, *Inca Architecture*, p. 320.

55. Gasparini and Margolies, *Inca Architecture*, p. 320.

Chapter 5: Survival of the Site

56. MSNBC News Services, "Peru's Inca Jewel," September 11, 2000. www.msnbc.com.

57. Quoted in CNN.com, "Sacred Stone in Machu Picchu Damaged During Beer Commercial," September 12, 2000. www.cnn.com.

58. Quoted in Amber Cook, "The Way to Machu Picchu," *Native Peoples*, March/April 2001.

59. Quoted in Cook, "The Way to Machu Picchu."

60. Richard Bangs, "Machu Picchu: On the Inca Trail, Part 3: Unraveling the Mysteries," www.msnbc.com/news/565493.asp.

61. Bangs, "Machu Picchu."

GLOSSARY

adobe: Bricks formed of mud and straw and dried in the sun; may have been used in the upper parts of Inca buildings.

ashlar: A stone cut and shaped for use in building walls; produced by the Incas without the use of iron tools.

citadel: A fortress or stronghold.

gable: The triangular end of a building; the top of the triangle forms a ridge with the roof.

huaca: An object or place sacred to the Incas; often a rock outcrop or cave, or a river, spring, or lake.

kancha: A group of buildings within a walled enclosure typical of Inca settlements; a compound.

lintel: A bar—consisting of stone in Inca buildings—that spans an opening such as a doorway; supports the weight of the structure above the opening.

masma: A rectangular building with one of its long sides open; common to Inca settlements.

masonry: Stonework; the Incas were masters of building with stone.

mit'a: A labor tax enforced by the Incas; literally means "a turn," that is, "labor by turns" (workers were enlisted for a set "turn" or rotation, in other words, a shift).

mortar: A mix of lime, sand, or cement binding together bricks or stones in buildings; absent in classic Inca architecture.

niche: A hollow in a wall; believed to be used for storage in Inca buildings.

pirca: A basic method of constructing walls with fieldstone and mortar; used by the Incas for terrace walls and more rustic buildings.

polygonal masonry: An architectural style featuring stone blocks with more than four sides; borrowed and developed by the Incas from earlier Andean peoples.

qollqa: An Inca granary or storehouse; unlike most Inca buildings, some were round rather than rectangular.

quarry: A source of building stone; to dig or remove stones from a quarry bed.

quipu: A system of knots and colored strings used by the Incas to record information, from tax accounts to historical events.

Sapa Inca: The Inca head of state, who was also the Incas' spiritual leader; believed to be semidivine.

terrace: A leveled field created by the Incas along the slopes of the Andes to increase agriculture in the region; the fill of soil constituting the field is supported by retaining walls.

thatch: Plant material, such as grasses, matted together to use as roofing material by the Incas and others.

For Further Reading

Elizabeth Gemming, *Lost City in the Clouds: The Discovery of Machu Picchu.* New York: Coward, McCann and Geoghegan, 1980. Novelistic retelling of Hiram Bingham's quest for the legendary Lost City of the Incas, leading to his discovery of Machu Picchu. Draws from Bingham's own writings, though dialogue is invented.

Fiona Macdonald, *Inca Town.* New York: Franklin Watts, 1998. Takes readers on a guided tour of a fifteenth-century Inca town. The town is based loosely on Cuzco, the capital city of the Inca Empire. Cleverly presents details such as weather and climate in a "Time-Traveler's Guide" at the back of the book. Plenty of illustrations.

Elizabeth Mann, *Machu Picchu.* New York: Mikaya Press, 2000. Brief narrative of the history of the Inca Empire offering speculation on the building of Machu Picchu. Vividly written and illustrated. Includes a pullout section reconstructing the layout of the city.

Philip Steele, *The Incas and Machu Picchu.* New York: Dillon Press, 1993. Thematic survey of Machu Picchu and its Inca builders. Presents a clear, if somewhat dry, discussion of archaeological findings and their implications. Provides a number of photographs of the site, plus an extensive glossary.

WORKS CONSULTED

BOOKS

Carmen Bernand, *The Incas: People of the Sun.* New York: Harry N. Abrams, 1994. Brief history of the Incas, vividly written and illustrated. A final section features writings of conquistadors and travelers as well as accounts of the natives themselves. Includes a chapter on the discovery of Machu Picchu.

Hiram Bingham, *In the Wonderland of Peru: The Work Accomplished by the Peruvian Expedition of 1912, Under the Auspices of Yale University and the National Geographic Society.* Washington, DC: National Geographic Society, 1913. Bingham's report on his second expedition to Peru, sponsored by the National Geographic Society and Yale University. Here he relates his team's clearing and excavation of the ruins at Machu Picchu. Particularly valuable for the 250 black-and-white photographs illustrating the text.

———, *Lost City of the Incas: The Story of Machu Picchu and Its Builders.* New York: Duell, Sloan and Pearce, 1948. Bingham recounts his various expeditions to Peru and discusses the results. While his theories on Machu Picchu's history have been discounted, his account of finding the site is fascinating and full of detail. Also worthwhile is his description of the Incas' building techniques.

Pedro de Cieza de León, *The Incas.* Translated by Harriet de Onis. Edited by Victor Wolfgang von Hagen. Norman: University of Oklahoma Press, 1959. Firsthand account of the Inca civilization, originally published in 1553. The author was a Spaniard who arrived in the New World as a boy of thirteen. Present-day historians continue to cite his chronicle of Inca life. Included are observations on architecture.

Richard Danbury, *The Inca Trail: Cuzco and Machu Picchu.* Hinhead, Surrey, UK: Trailblazer Publications, 2000. A thorough guide to exploring these two Inca cities and the trail linking them. Provides site descriptions as well as plenty of background information on the ruins as they stand today. Offers insight into the Incas and their Andean predecessors.

Editors of Time-Life Books, *Incas: Lords of Gold and Glory*. Alexandria, VA: Time-Life Books, 1992. Fully illustrated survey of Inca history and culture. Includes brief sections on Machu Picchu and Inca stonework. Very readable and informative.

Val Jon Farris, *Inca Fire! Light of the Masters: A True and Inspiring Spiritual Adventure*. Auburn, CA: Keystone Group, 1999. An account of the author's spiritual revelations at Machu Picchu while on a pilgrimage there. Offers a New Age perspective on the meaning of the ruins, as well as a report on the site in contemporary times.

Graziano Gasparini and Luise Margolies, *Inca Architecture*. Translated by Patricia J. Lyon. Bloomington: Indiana University Press, 1980. A comprehensive study of the form and development of Inca architecture, first published in Spanish. The authors, experts in pre-Columbian art and architecture, are based in South America. Lots of explanatory drawings and diagrams are provided.

John Hemming, *Machu Picchu*. New York: Newsweek, 1981. Spotlights the search for the legendary Lost City of the Incas resulting in the discovery of Machu Picchu. Also presents an overview of Inca culture. Concludes with a selection of literary works inspired by the monument.

———, *Monuments of the Incas*. Boston: Little, Brown, 1982. A photographic study of Inca sites emphasizing their integration with the natural environment. One chapter is devoted to Machu Picchu. Another examines characteristics of Inca architecture.

John Hyslop, *Inka Settlement Planning*. Austin: University of Texas Press, 1990. An investigation into how Inca settlements were designed and their sites selected, with occasional reference to Machu Picchu. Presents varying viewpoints supported by archaeological evidence. Scholarly, but with plenty of photographs, maps, and diagrams.

Max Milligan, *Realm of the Incas*. New York: Universe Publishing, 2001. With a masterful eye for the region's unstinting beauty and mystery, photojournalist Milligan records his journey through the lands surrounding Cuzco at the heart of the Inca Empire. An entire chapter is devoted to Machu Picchu.

Michael A. Milpass, *Daily Life in the Inca Empire.* Westport, CT: Greenwood Press, 1996. A survey of Inca culture and society, placed in historical context. Very brief discussion of architecture and construction techniques; more valuable for imagining the activity taking place in and around Inca buildings.

Kenneth R. Wright and Alfredo Valencia Zegarra, *Machu Picchu: A Civil Engineering Marvel.* Reston, VA: American Society of Civil Engineers Press, 2000. Wright, an engineer, and Zegarra, an archaeologist, set out to investigate the water-engineering practices of the builders of Machu Picchu. The authors' on-site research expanded to include agricultural practices, stonework, and construction methods.

PERIODICALS

Bill Allen, "From the Editor," *National Geographic Magazine* 198:2 (August 2000).

Amber Cook, "The Way to Machu Picchu," *Native Peoples*, March/April 2001.

Mark Holston, "Reseeding a Singed Inca City," *Américas*, January/February 1998.

Keith Kachtick, "Invisible Incas," *Texas Monthly*, May 1996.

VIDEO

Allen Abel, *Machu Picchu: Secrets of the Inca Empire.* Time-Life Video; a CineNova Production for the Discovery Channel, 1999.

INTERNET SOURCES

Richard Bangs, "Machu Picchu: On the Inca Trail, Part 3: Unraveling the Mysteries." www.msnbc.com. The author's observations on a visit to Machu Picchu since it became a tourist attraction. Bangs questions whether the crowds flocking to the site are in danger of breaking its spell.

Sally Bowen, "Bringing the Inca Canals Back to Life." www. oneworld.org. A report on archaeologist Ann Kendall's mission to restore Inca irrigation canals with the goal of reviving rural communities outside Cuzco.

Susan Litherland, "Peru: Ancient Irrigation Works Restored to Raise Record Crops." www.interlog.com. Litherland reports on archaeologist Ann Kendall's founding of the Cusichaca Trust and the success of Trust projects in reconstructing Inca irrigation systems.

Elías J. Mujica, "Machu Picchu." World Heritage Review 11. www.unesco.org. Presents brief overview of the National Historical Sanctuary of Machu Picchu and lobbies for its continued preservation.

WEBSITES

GeoZoo: Spectacled Bear. (www.geobop.com) Provides general information on the spectacled bear's appearance, behavior, and interaction with human populations. Brief, clear presentation.

The New 7 Wonders of the World Project. (www.newsevenwonders. com) Presents goal and scope of the project to name Seven New Wonders of the contemporary world. Selections were open to a vote logged on the site.

The Spectacled Bear Website. (www.cecalc.ula.ve) Field researchers Isaac Goldstein and Denis Alexander Torres developed the site to inform the public about the history and habits of the spectacled bear, as well as efforts to conserve the endangered animal. Many images provided.

INDEX

civil war among, 20–21
disease epidemic among, 19–20
downfall of, 22
empire of, 12
establishment of, 10
food distribution of, 82
religion of, 42, 81–82
road system of, 62–64
royalty of, 39–40
tax system of, 51
Incas: Lords of Gold and Glory, 37
Inca Trail, 39, 64, 90, 94
Industrial Group, 17
Instituto Nacional de Cultura (National Institute of Culture), 86
Inti (god), 16, 23, 35, 37, 44, 46
Intihuatana, 17, 44, 85–86
Intipunku (Gate of the Sun), 38
iron, 50

kallankas, 76–77
kancha, 79
Kendall, Ann, 60

labor force, 51–52
León, Pedro de Cieza de, 74
llulli, 46
locks, 80–81
Lost City of the Incas. *See* Vilcabamba

Machu Picchu
abandonment of, 18–21
burial sites at, 31–33
commercial use of, 85–86
discovery of, 24–29
excavation of, 28–33
hanansaya of, 16–17
huacas at, 42–43
hurinsaya of, 17–18
isolation of, 21–22, 24
location of, 16
planning of, 47–49
preservation of, 86–95
purpose of, 34–42
roads to, 62–64
stonework of, 27–28, 33, 68–73
sun temple of, 43–44
theories about, 12, 34–42
    New Age, 45–46
    religious significance, 42–45
    was *acllas* shelter, 35
    was built by Pachacuti, 40–42
    was citadel, 35–38
    was sanctuary, 39–40
    was Vilcabamba, 34–35
tourism to, 14–15, 89–95
see also architecture; construction
Machu Picchu (Hemming), 30, 41
MacLean, Margaret Greenup, 43
maize, 74
mamaconas, 37
Mama Huaca, 74
Mama-Quilla (goddess), 23
Manrique, Gustavo, 86

PICTURE CREDITS

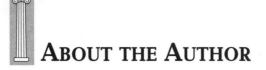

ABOUT THE AUTHOR

Machu Picchu is Amy Allison's second title for the Building History series. She also wrote *Shakespeare's Globe.* Allison's other books on architectural subjects include *Gargoyles on Guard.* She earned her bachelor's degree from the University of California, Santa Barbara, and her master's from the Pacific School of Religion in Berkeley, California, where she studied spirituality and the arts. Allison now lives in the Los Angeles area.